A Guide to

MANGA, ANIME
and VIDEO GAME
COSPLAY

Breeze Dancer – *Naruto Online.*

A Guide to
MANGA, ANIME and VIDEO GAME COSPLAY

Holly Swinyard

WHITE OWL

AN IMPRINT OF PEN & SWORD BOOKS LTD.
YORKSHIRE – PHILADELPHIA

Thanks to Meg Amis, Margaret Swinyard, Dominic Westerland, Helen McCarthy,
Jemma Le Pelley and the cosplayers of the UK

First published in Great Britain in 2022 by
White Owl
An imprint of
Pen & Sword Books Ltd
Yorkshire - Philadelphia

Typeset in 11/15 pts Sabon by
SJmagic DESIGN SERVICES, India.

Printed and bound in India by Replika Press Pvt. Ltd.

Pen & Sword Books Ltd incorporates the imprints of Pen & Sword Books
Archaeology, Atlas, Aviation, Battleground, Discovery, Family History, History,
Maritime, Military, Naval, Politics, Railways, Select, Transport, True Crime, Fiction,
Frontline Books, Leo Cooper, Praetorian Press, Seaforth Publishing, Wharncliffe and
White Owl.

For a complete list of Pen & Sword titles please contact

PEN & SWORD BOOKS LIMITED
47 Church Street, Barnsley, South Yorkshire, S70 2AS, England
E-mail: enquiries@pen-and-sword.co.uk
Website: www.pen-and-sword.co.uk

or

PEN AND SWORD BOOKS
1950 Lawrence Rd, Havertown, PA 19083, USA
E-mail: Uspen-and-sword@casematepublishers.com
Website: www.penandswordbooks.com

Contents

Vox Machina – *Critical Role Campaign One.*

What is Cosplay?

Introduction

Have you ever wanted to find a magical gem that transforms you into a super-powered space princess? Or wished you could be whisked away to a castle in the sky to be a mysterious wizard? Just found yourself turning a broken branch into a wand while you're doing your weekly shop? Then you should keep reading this book and take a moment to come into the wonderful world of escapism, artistic crafts and fantastical creations that is cosplay.

Just by picking up this book it says that you, or someone you know, is interested in cosplay. You're drawn to that little spark of creativity and adventure that it promises. Maybe you are thinking 'I wish I could try that' or 'I loved dressing up when I was little' and you're wondering if you can get involved. Or possibly you are someone who already loves the lexicon of craft, media and storytelling that defines the world of cosplay and wants to find more about it. Well, this book, and its twin (*A Guide to Film and TV Cosplay*), are little portals for anyone who wants to take a look at cosplay and everything that goes with it. Maybe you'll even decide to stay for a bit.

In the last few years more and more cosplay has appeared in the mainstream, on sitcoms, in the news, in video games and comic books and manga, it's all over YouTube and streaming services, there have even documentaries about it – but why is it so popular? What is it that draws people in and inspires them to make these amazing costumes?

The thing is, that with cosplay, and costuming hobbies like it, you are opening the door to a whole myriad of experiences, skills and ideas without having to worry about what to do with them or how to apply them to some sort of real-life situation. It's all just for fun.

You don't need to 'hustle' with cosplay – unless you want to – or do anything more than just add joy to your life for the sake of your own creative expression and the want to do something fun because it's fun. As adults we can often find ourselves thinking 'But what's the point in doing this? Is it productive?', when we should be thinking 'Am I having fun? Am I doing something because it makes me happy?'

There is so much telling us that we have to do things in the right way, that there are certain rules to stick to, that we need to colour inside the lines to make something beautiful, and as more and more rules get placed on us we start to forget that play is important. We can start telling ourselves it's embarrassing that we enjoy things. How many worry that we still like cartoons or playing board games or enjoying alternative fashion now that we've passed our childhood years? But we really shouldn't do that to ourselves. If something infuses you with a passion, then let it be part of your life. Enjoy it. Fantasy is no bad thing and playing make-believe is just as valid at 40 as it is at four.

There is a reason that nerd culture is on the rise. People are remembering how much fun it is to play Dungeons and Dragons or watch superhero movies. We all need a little bit of escapism. Embrace your inner child and take a deep dive into cosplay.

Dressing up and making costumes is the most wonderful form of make-believe, feeding your brain with creativity, teaching yourself new skills and opening up your space to new experiences. It takes you to places where you can be who you've always dreamed of being. Wearing that costume can open your eyes to new things about yourself as well as new experiences. You might just look like Sailor Moon for a day, but you never know, some of that character may well rub off on you in other aspects of your life too. Cosplay can really give you a new sense of self and inner strength. Powerful thing, playing.

Part of the joy of cosplay is that you get to find and define how you want to interact with it as a hobby. There are so many different routes into cosplay, from different media and mediums to different ways to make, wear and be the characters you love, and you get to pick and mix however you want. There are no finite rules that you have to stay within; you don't have to colour inside the lines to have fun.

Mercy, Soldier 76, and Ana – *Overwatch*.

What is Cosplay?

So you think you know what cosplay is? You've seen it on social media or on TV, and it's dressing up as your favourite characters, building ridiculous costumes and props, and going to comic book conventions as Captain America, right? That's it in a nutshell, but there's a little bit more to the story than that. The moment you take that deep breath and dive past the surface you can see that this is the tip of the cosplay iceberg. There are so many more facets to this unusual hobby than simply being a more extreme version of fancy dress.

Ask anyone involved in cosplay what it is to them and you will probably get as many answers as people you ask. For some, cosplay is as simple as dressing up on the weekends for a laugh, but for others it's about finding a space to be themselves, even if that means being someone else for the day. For many people it's about community and connecting with likeminded individuals, whilst for others it is about learning skills and crafts and passing on that knowledge. Some may see it as art, some may be there for competition, and some may simply want a new way to tell and appreciate the stories they love. Each way of thinking about cosplay is correct and valid in its own right, and they all build up to the picture of what cosplay is.

What connects all of this, and each different experience of cosplay, is the love for the characters. The costumes might be what is worn on the outside, but what's important to cosplayers is becoming and embodying the characters. It's a way of sticking your colours to the mast and showing people what you care about. It could be seen as wearing your team's football strip to support them. If you love something, why not literally wear it on your sleeve? That's what the early pioneers of cosplay thought.

Cosplay as a hobby has been around for a lot longer than you might think. If one were to guess, a lot of people might think it first turned up in the 1980s, and you would be half right. The word cosplay did come into existence then but cosplay itself had been kicking around the pop culture sphere for a good 40 years before the name itself was invented. This is not some fad brought about by the internet, though no one can argue that technology has not been a huge boon to the hobby, but it is a long-standing tradition of those who are a touch more nerd minded.

It's arguable that it is actually even older, with the first costumes that could be called cosplay appearing at the turn of the twentieth century. But is that even the beginning of it all? Humans have been dressing up and acting as characters for social and communal reasons since there have been humans. We are creatures who love to tell stories and inhabit the characters within them. Think of the carnivals of Venice or the masked balls of European royalty. The costumes that were worn at those events were the well-known characters (or caricatures) of their day. They were the equivalent of pop culture; they were the *popular* culture. If you remove the blinkers of these taking place in a historical period or a classical setting you can see that there is a very clear, direct link between these parties, balls, or masquerades and the modern cosplay that we do today.

You can go all the way back to storytellers of ancient and prehistoric times and draw lines through every type of mask-wearing, character-inhabiting, fancy-dressing form of

Ozymandias – *Fate/ Grand Order.*

entertainment humans have ever enjoyed to cosplay. It might sound a little corny but cosplay is very much a progression of the costuming art.

One of the joys of all types of costuming from any time period is that you get to be someone else for a little while, or to express elements of yourself that you normally are afraid to let out. For a lot of cosplayers, this is the reason why they do it, so they can be both seen and not seen, anonymous but recognised by everyone. It's a wonderful way to gain confidence in yourself as a person, and you can practice building and having that confidence in plain sight. When you pick a character, you drape part of their personality around yourself, affecting you as a person and making it part of yourself. That was the whole point of the Venice Carnival, to be whoever you wanted to be and break out of your normal role and rules for a brief moment in time. Doesn't that describe cosplay to a tee?

Pop culture is at the heart of so much of modern life so it is hardly surprising that we choose to see ourselves in those characters in the same way that our ancestors would take on the roles of the characters that lived at the centre of their society. Gods and goddesses, kings, queens and fools, heroes of legend and creatures from myth. Movies, comics, fantasy and science fiction: they're modern mythology, modern folk lore, built on the shoulders of those same stories that our ancestors told and related to.

The same archetypes, the same story themes, the same lessons to learn, just told in a new way. If ancient people used masks and animal hides in firelight to bring the stories of heroes to life, or shadow puppets with a magic lantern, then of course we feel the same way about sitting in the cinema. The characters that we see walking around Comic Con could very easily be the *Comedia De'Arte* characters who ran rampant through the streets of Venice during Carnival, or storytellers bringing *Beowulf* to life with masks. We have comic cons and Renaissance faires instead of the masquerade balls (though we should definitely consider having more fancy-dress balls) but they are fundamentally the same thing. (See *A Guide to Film and TV Cosplay* for more information on this).

This is a large part of the reason why cosplay is so popular on a global scale: because it already was. And has been for a long time. It's a global experience. Costume making and crafting has a root in every country in the world, and using costume in storytelling professionally or just for fun is found everywhere. It's no surprise that this modern form is springing up all over the place. People want to make things, they want to be characters, they want to connect to each other through shared loves and they want to be a little bit silly.

Makes cosplay sound pretty cool when you think about it like that.

What's wonderful is that cosplay is not just carrying on the tradition of costume as a storytelling and cultural practice, but it is also making sure that traditional crafts are kept alive as well. Cosplayers are part of a global movement to save and restore traditional crafts that are disappearing. Leatherwork, smithing, embroidery, weaving, felting, woodwork and many other traditional crafts are being taken up by cosplayers and other costumers to add to their own skill sets, and by doing so they are bringing them back to life. And they encourage others to engage with restoration too.

Plenty of cosplayers and other costume makers are building up businesses and crafting practices around traditional skills because there is a demand for them. Other cosplayers want to buy and commission work, people from other costuming hobbies might need a historically accurate sword belt or want a LARP (Live Action Role Play) -safe arrow fletched in a traditional fashion. Cosplayers have even been known to supply large scale costuming houses for TV and film since they are the ones who have the crafting know-how. But these traditional craftspeople aren't just keeping it to themselves either. A lot of them have started doing classes, tutorials and writing books on the subject to reach out into the community and teach others.

The joy of this is, if you think some leather armour looks cool and you want to try it for your next costume, the cosplayer who made it is likely to be able to tell you how to do it, or at the very least point you in the right direction to start learning yourself. Cosplayers have latched onto the idea of community learning, whether they realise it or not. Educating each other through sharing knowledge online or in person, and creating crafting groups to encourage each other and themselves to try new things with someone there to hold your hand through the process is an unexpected benefit.

This is one of the elements at the core of traditional crafting and one of the best ways to save it. Communities thrive like this as well, as when each member becomes more knowledgeable and more confident in passing that knowledge onto the next person they can grow in both size and productivity. Cosplayers are masters of this. Part of what it means to be a cosplayer is to share your skills and your knowledge, whether that's through one-to-one conversations or through creating tutorials or running classes for anyone who wants to learn. Sharing crafting skills and media across cultures and countries shows cosplay in new and different ways, helping build a global community.

As with anything that stretches over cultural borders there are going to be things within the hobby that don't quite match up from one subgroup to the next. Every country and community will have its own ways of doing things, affected by the culture of that community outside of cosplay. But they will all have similarities as well. Europe is different from America, America is different from Asia, different areas of Asia are different from each other, and even different countries or states within a country can have a different culture of cosplay norms. It's great to see and learn how everyone is adding their own ideas to the hobby and to cross the streams a bit, bringing those ideas from one culture to another.

Despite the global nature of cosplay, there is still a belief in a lot of modern nerd culture that it originated in Japan, but this, much in the same way that people believe cosplay hasn't been around that long, is a misconception. The myth of cosplay being a solely Japanese invention is probably due to the fact that the word cosplay did come from Japan; coined by a Japanese journalist to describe what he had seen at an American convention in 1984. Add in the well-known aesthetic presence of manga and anime in the world of cosplay and you have an easily believed and spread myth.

Cosplay as a concept, as a community and a hobby has grown and continued to blend into a multicultural and global creation over the 90 years since its conception. Even before the ease of communication that the internet brought about, costume

Jiraiya — *Naruto.*

makers were spreading the good word from convention to convention and country to country through fanzines and newsletters, or in person. It wasn't fast, but it worked, not only bringing together many different media, mediums and methodology from all over the world but also people, to become what we know today.

While you may have a shock seeing how cosplayers do things in Japan, it's a bit like reading a manga for the first time after reading comic books your whole life. The same thing, it just looks a bit different. And you may have some things backwards.

For example, in Europe and the US it's incredibly common for cosplayers to ride on public transport and travel to an event in costume, as well as to go and get food or go for a drink afterwards still dressed up, whereas in Japan that is completely unheard of. In fact it would be shocking to do that. The bigger Japanese conventions tend to have a separate area for cosplayers to gather in costume, do photos and films, sometimes with predesignated times for certain things, and participants don't go into the event in costume at all.

Linkle – *The Legend of Zelda: Hyrule Warriors Legends.*

It's also more common for Japanese cosplayers to buy their costumes rather than make them, since Japanese people, especially in cities, often don't have the space to

craft in their own homes. In the US people have huge amounts of space, with many cosplayers having garages turned into workshops or a spare room they can use, so crafting your own stuff is seen as more achievable, even if that isn't the case for other reasons like finances.

In Europe cosplay competitions can run for hours and hours, and there are plenty of anecdotes of them running late into the night, whereas in the UK they can be done and dusted in a couple of hours at most. These are all different ways to approach the hobby due to culture and country, but they are still all definitely cosplay. The differences are small compared to the similarities. You can recognise the same enjoyment of the artistry and creativity in the costumes and the wearing of them, and the same love of character and storytelling.

It all comes back to that, no matter what lens you use to look at cosplay through. All the crafting, stitching, hot glue burns, and empty wallets come back to the love of character. That's why so many different subcultures of pop culture meet under the umbrella of cosplay.

There are little threads of cosplay in almost every pop culture and costuming pie in the world at this point. Mediums like video games, manga and anime have attracted a large following of cosplayers due to their interesting and often unique storytelling styles as well as innovative artistic aesthetic, costume design and character portrayal.

It is hard to ignore the way that anime and manga has influenced cosplay. There is a reason that when people think of cosplaying, the first image to jump into their head is of kawaii characters with oversized swords and gravity defying hair. Anime and manga have had a growing popularity since the 80s outside of Japan, with anime like *Pokémon* and the Studio Ghibli films becoming cultural icons across the world.

Manga and anime brought a completely different aesthetic to cosplay, which had up until the 1980s been dominated by the likes of *Star Trek* and science fiction in general since its conception. Manga exploded onto the US and European cosplay scenes with a bang, enthralling cosplayers and pop culture lovers alike with its more dramatic stylisation and different storytelling traditions. The art style and narratives of the American Marvel and DC comics stood in stark contrast to the imagery and stories that were being told on the pages of manga books or in the anime series that every 90s kid remembers.

Sailor Moon and *Dragon Ball Z* have a lot to answer for in creating a generation of cosplayers inspired by the colourful costumes and explosive stories of princesses, aliens, superpowers and friendship. And modern manga and anime is doing much the same, with series like *My Hero Academia* and *Attack on Titan* pulling a whole new generation into the world of cosplay.

The evolution of video games has also had a massive effect on cosplay as a hobby and its overall popularity. Going from the basic *Pong*-type games up to self-insert, open-world storytelling has made it so you can be part of an interactive film with all the elements of movies, books, comics and TV shows, but you're the main character. It would be a little odd if games hadn't inspired people to create costumes on the level they do. And since more people are playing video games than ever before, there are more people

Ejiro Kirishma – *My Hero Academia.*

Chosen Undead – *Dark Souls.*

who are seeing these costumes on social media, often promoted by the companies, and wanting to get involved themselves. Games companies know this so some have even made designing characters to be attractive to cosplayers part of their thought process when creating a new game.

It is very common for major games to have multiple different skins for the playable characters in the game, or a huge amount of choice in character creation for designing your own avatar within the game. These factors are selling points for the game but also they are very appealing to cosplayers wanting to try something different with a character they love. It isn't unheard of for cosplayers to be involved in the design process, or at the very least give feedback on a design to see if it will be of interest to that area of the market. Large gaming companies such as Bethesda, Ubisoft and Blizzard have all employed cosplayers to promote their games, getting them to make and cosplay as the most recognisable or exciting characters at conventions or on social media.

But it's not all in the hands of the big players (pun intended), and cosplayers will always find their way to the most innovative form of storytelling out there. It is incredibly hard to break into mainstream games design, TV production or film. A lot of new creators have moved away from these more 'traditional' forms of media in favour of telling new stories and creating new aesthetics in other ways, through the freedom of the internet.

Games and sequential storytelling can be created in an online sphere relatively cheaply and with far fewer people involved in a project. It could just be one person working on a game and it could become hugely popular. Perfect examples of this happening are the webcomic *Homestuck* and the retro style game *Undertale,* which both gained mass

Mettaton – *Undertale*.

followings online due to unusual and dynamic storytelling, but without ever having to go through mainstream channels.

This leads to innovation in all areas of these media as the mainstream in turn wants to 'get in on the action', and other creators and companies want to push the boundaries of their own stories to find a similar level of following. And cosplayers are drawn to these weird and wonderful things like moths to a flame. There was a time when you couldn't move at Comic Con for people cosplaying from *Homestuck*.

Webcomics and original online creations have also inspired new levels of creativity in cosplayers. The stories that are told in these projects aren't subject to boardrooms of editors and production teams making sure that the project will be profitable, which often leads to minority groups being unrepresented in the mainstream. This mentality doesn't arise in these smaller projects. A lot of webcomics feature people of colour as leads, LGBTQIA+ characters and relationships are given centre stage, as are people with disabilities. And it means that cosplayers in those minority groups see themselves in ways that they might not do in other forms of media. This media is transformative in the same way that cosplay is and shines a light on a multitude of stories that can be told.

Player Character
Original Design –
*Dungeons and
Dragons.*

This desire to see more diverse characters may also explain the massive shift towards more media like tabletop role play games, either playing them yourself or watching streamed games. It's a completely different way of telling stories, often in huge winding epics reminiscent of oral storytelling traditions of the past, or *The Lord of the Rings*, and have common elements and themes, common character archetypes, and the common thread of people coming together to enjoy the story and create together. Cosplayers have in recent years begun to take this form of storytelling to heart and blend together the two hobbies in the best way they know how: by making costumes.

Though most people play with their friends and family just for fun, some of these games have moved online into the realms of Twitch and YouTube, as well as other streaming services, to tell their stories to a wider audience and create their own fanbases. Not only does this generate people who are fans of the gaming shows and the stories that are being played through the medium of tabletop role playing games, but also creates new fans of the style of gameplay itself. It is unsurprising that people want to recreate the stories that they are creating in costume form. *Dungeons and Dragons* can get pretty emotionally charged – you think this is a joke, but you just wait until your character gets killed off!

These ideas of character creation and telling stories that are just for you and your friends created in an organic oral tradition, has spilled over into people making characters of their own purely just to cosplay as them. Not dissimilar to LARP, this type of cosplaying is becoming popular on online platforms such as TikTok, where global communication has allowed for large scale collaboration. But you don't even have to do it with other people. You can start bringing your ideas to life on your own, build your own worlds and draw others into your fantastical tales through costume and performance, just the same as in any other cosplay.

You don't have to like everything that is brought together in this nerdy web. Not everyone is going to find anime charming or care about playing a roleplaying game that literally lasts for years, but cosplay makes you aware and appreciative of all these different ways of crafting stories. Most cosplayers will have pretty good general knowledge of almost every nerd related subculture there is, purely by osmosis. You may have no idea who that character is, or what they are from, but you've walked past five people dressed as them in the time it took you to get into the convention hall. You'll probably find you actually know something about them and the show they are from, and you didn't even realise. Goes to show how powerful a medium for sharing new stories cosplay can be.

Alice – *Alice: Madness Returns.*

At the heart of it, cosplay, as with any artistic hobby, is about storytelling. From the literal discussion of the media that the costumes come from to the stories told by those who choose to be part of the community. Each costume, each prop, each video on social media has an element of storytelling that is unparalleled. The stories that people remember, that they want to dress up and celebrate are the ones that make them brave, comfort them, and tell them they can be and do anything they want; they are the ones that help people learn about themselves and about who they want to be. That's what cosplay is.

And sometimes it's dressing up as Captain America.

A Very Brief History of Manga and its Link to Cosplay

Cosplay and Japan are intrinsically linked in the landscape of modern pop culture. If you think of cosplay, one of the first things to come to mind is people dressed as anime characters. The costumes are often bright and dramatic with amazing wigs and oversized props; there are the cute sports anime costumes and magical girl uniforms, or the spooky kids in a zombie horror and the serious samurai from more traditional manga stories, and of course anything and everything in between.

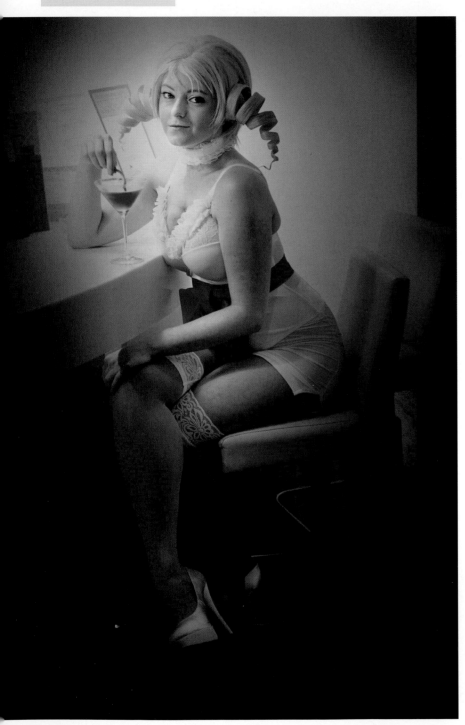

Catherine – *Catherine*.

But why is it that we often think of Japan when we first think about cosplay? How is it that manga, anime and the Japanese gaming industry have become so linked with cosplay that it took the explosion of media based on the more 'classic' costuming fodder of Marvel Comics and the *Star Wars* franchise to unseat manga from its throne? There was a point when if you thought of cosplay in Europe and America most people would equate manga and cosplay as being one and the same thing. Did all of this just happen out of sheer coincidence or is there something about the way that Japan and cosplay became intertwined that shows there is more to it.

The history of cosplay in Japan is completely tied to the history of manga. This was, and still is, the most popular medium and form of pop culture in Japan, on par with the popularity of television and film in the US and Europe. Manga and anime are now well known all over the world; the stylistic use of imagery and designs of kawaii characters is universally being used as an international language of sorts by Japan to advertise itself to the world. The Japanese foreign office has used famous manga artists to help recruit people to work with them and to encourage tourists to visit Japan. Manga has been a very successful way of putting Japan on the global stage, but this was not always the case.

As with any culture you have to know how the foundations were put in place to continue building it into something that will last, and with cosplay growing to be a bigger and bigger hobby everyday thanks to things like social media, knowing where it came from and the influences that make it what it is will help us celebrate it all the more.

To understand cosplay in Japan, and by extension its connection with Japanese pop culture, it is important to first understand Japanese pop culture and traditional methods of art and storytelling.

Early Manga and Sequential Art

It may be the popular face of Japan to the rest of the world now, but manga has a much deeper history in Japanese culture than just *Dragon Ball Z*, *Pokemon* and cutesy mascots. Much like cosplay, modern manga is the product of Japanese art forms and ideas colliding with American and European ones in an explosion of creativity. The influence of studios like Disney are obvious when you look for them. Those large, cartoonish eyes that manga is known for nowadays aren't found in Japanese art in the same way before the 20th century, when the likes of *Betty Boop* and *Mickey Mouse* were taking the whole world by storm. This being said, manga, and storytelling through pictorial imagery have been a major part of Japanese culture for centuries in a very distinct way, as opposed to the European and American understanding of comics and cartooning.

Sheik – *The Legend of Zelda: Ocarina of Time.*

Before we fully dive into the history of manga and anime, let's just explain what they mean. Manga is the Japanese form of comics, being sequential art that tells and story, and anime is animated storytelling, cartoons in western terms. Got it? Ok, let's go!

Sequential images have been important in Japanese culture since the 1100s; small, hand painted scrolls of text and images were popular, as were much larger, illustrated hanging scrolls in this period. Both could easily be seen as being precursors to modern manga, and actually were used to bring more widespread literacy in the populace - using images meant that the narrative of the text was simpler to understand. In fact comics and manga are used to this day as a way to teach literacy; sometimes the old ways really do work best.

In the 1600s books called *Toba-e* started to appear in Japan becoming incredibly popular, incredibly quickly. These basic but, amusing picture books, that could be gotten hold of with very little effort, aided in the continuing education of the Japanese people throughout this period and helped increase the literacy of the population so that not only wealthy or higher-class people were reading. The population was obsessed with these books which meant that the popularity of novels continued to grow. By the 1700s comic novels (as in funny, though also they were of the illustrated variety) were being printed in *huge* quantities to fulfil the increasingly high demand. As printing technology evolved, more books could be printed, the interest rose, so more books were in demand, so more books printed, ad infinitum.

This in turn lead to satirical comics (this time illustrated type, but also funny) and social commentary starting to be seen in Japan. It's around this time that some of those who can really be called the first manga artists come to the forefront, such as Santō Kyōden, known for his exaggeration and literary wordplay, and more specialized publishers who would begin changing manga to make it appear more like it does today.

It is during the 1600s that Kabuki theatre appears as well. If you're looking for an origin story for modern anime, complete with vengeance, sword fights and more over the top drama than you can shake a stick at, then Kabuki is where you want to be!

Known for its dramatic storytelling and stylization, Kabuki used, and still uses, exaggerated costumes, masks and make-up to bring the characters and stories to life in a way that many modern anime lovers would know better than the back of their own hand. Much like the printed form of storytelling, people loved the larger-than-life performances and the art form developed throughout the 1600s and 1700s.

Many of the Kabuki stories featured samurai and their deeds, not unlike the stories of knights and dragons that were common in Europe at the time (humans do love a tale of derring-do, don't we), but since impersonating a samurai or members of the ruling class in any way was illegal the performers went out of their way to design elaborate costumes and props to represent them instead.

Brightly coloured and made from many, many, *many* layers of fabric, Kabuki costumes exaggerated every aspect of the characters. Along with stylized masks and makeup to invoke animal like or supernatural imagery in the minds of the audience, this trend of stylization left its mark on Japanese artistic styles; much of it would not be out of place if seen in modern manga and anime.

However, one of the biggest turning points for the development of modern manga didn't come until a century later, in the 1860s. It's at this point when Japan, which been a closed nation for over 200 years, was opening up to more international trade and ideas. People from all over the world started settling in Japan, and brought with them the game changer, the thing that would skyrocket manga into the future. That's right, it's the big one, the daily newspaper. And with it, serialized comic strips.

The cartoon strips that featured in the new, more western style, newspapers included recognizable characters that continued from week to week; soon many manga artists found themselves in demand outside of the country by papers due to their artistic ability. One such artist was Kitazawa Rakuten who was hired by the paper *Box of Curios* in Australia, drawing in (a pun? In this book? Surely not) new worldwide interest in Japanese art in a whole new way.

But it was the founding of the newspaper *Jiji shinpō* that cemented this new format. It contained manga as a part of the paper in a more prominent position than ever before, filling a whole supplement with manga, and was the first to use the word manga as the title of the strips.

It doesn't feel like a surprise that Kabuki also saw a revival in interest during this time. The 1860s saw mass change happening on a cultural level and the Japanese samurai class had all but disappeared. However, the desire to retain the traditions and knowledge of the samurai as more and more foreign influence was felt across the country spurred actors, playwriters and theatres to bring Kabuki back in a way that both celebrated and modernized the art form, giving traditional stories a much more contemporary touch.

This massive swell in creativity and technological progression spurred manga artists on to new heights. They couldn't be held back. Many started to develop their own styles, looking to American and European comics for inspiration, blending these styles with the classic Japanese art forms that they knew and loved. This was a time of experimentation and excitement;

Ty Lee – *Avatar: The Last Airbender.*

the first society for manga artists was started, called Nippon Mangakai, and schools to teach manga as an art form appeared for young artists to learn the emerging craft. Over the turn of the 20th century manga was growing; going from strength to strength and gaining in popularity beyond what could ever have been expected. People loved the little stories and the characters that they could keep up with week on week. There were little worlds to dip into for five minutes before getting on with day to day life.

Ty Lee – *Avatar: The Last Airbender.*

But this period of boom was about to go bust.

World War II and its fall out had a devastating effect on Japan and its people.

During the war, the Japanese government kept a tight hold on what information was published and many of the publications that had been so supportive and promising for manga disappeared over night.

Those magazines that managed to survive were used to support the war effort, and patriotic messages were spread through the manga. The press was hijacked, and manga became one of the easiest ways to put across the government's ideas to the populous at large. Only those magazines that were deemed appropriate and helpful were allowed to be published, and this control over the press continued after the war, as the American forces occupied and took tighter hold of the reins of censorship than ever before. This monitoring would not end until 1952.

Post War to 1970s

The strict post war censorship laws that were put in place stopped any critique of the US and the other Allied Forces in Japanese media of any sort. Anything that the censors deemed to be "subversive" material, which included the glorification of war and the Japanese military, was prohibited from public release. However, this was not an outright ban on publications and the manga scene that had been flourishing before the war found a way to recover.

Manga, which was seen as "childish", often slipped through the net of censorship. Comics in America had very much become the domain of children, so artists saw manga as a way to discuss political ideas and the intense shared experiences of the Japanese people without being picked up by the censors. Hopefully.

A new, sneakier, era of manga blossomed under the very noses of the American occupiers, with creative flare of the artists forced to evolve as they worked to think outside the box to keep the supply of manga coming.

The shōjo manga, or girls' manga titled *Sazae-san* was one of those manga that made its way through to be published in 1949.

It told the stories of Sazae, a young woman and the struggles of living in the modern world of Tokyo. While on the surface you could excuse this manga as a slice of life, the stories were full of meaning between the lines. Here was an honest representation of many Japanese people who struggled after the war, but Sazae's happiness and resilience as a character shone through despite hardships. *Sazae-san* showed kindness and humour in a time when many needed it, and lead to it becoming one of the most popular manga to ever be published. It was so popular, if truth be told, that the anime, which started in 1969, was still being aired in 2020. One of the longest running in history!

But don't worry if you aren't into the more down to Earth stories, this period also saw the creation of Shōnen, or boys' comics, which tended to head more into the action adventure and science fiction areas of the story telling spectrum. This brought about two distinctly different styles of manga. Though they were considered for boys and girls separately when they were conceived, this distinction has most definitely blurred over time. Nowadays it is more the stylization and the methods of storytelling for shōnen and shōjo that define them, and these have stayed much the same as those used from the start.

The most popular and long lasting shōnen manga of this early period is *Astro Boy*. If you know anything about manga, and even if you don't, *Astro Boy* is iconic through pop culture, having been rebooted in different mediums more times than you can count; new manga, anime and even films have been made right up to the 2010s.

Like *Sazae-san, Astro Boy* spoke to a generation of people in Japan as an escape from the patriotic and militarized manga of the pre-war period. Both in their own way focused on community and the title character's attempts at navigating family, friends and love as well as their adventures. It was ordinary in the most extraordinary way, which is what Japan needed. These manga spoke to people, and from 1950 onwards both genres of manga flourished. But it was shōjo, and the army of young women who had fallen in love with the medium of manga, that was about to shake things up, and lead to one of the first glimpses of cosplay in Japan.

Cosplays from Katsucon and Animazement 1980s and 1990s, dates unknown.

This change up came in the form of fashion illustrations of all things. They featured heavily in women's magazines at the time and shōjo artists became increasingly inspired by them. Full body images of characters in the latest fashion styles started to appear in shōjo, encouraging women to make themselves look like their favourites. One artist, Junichi Nakahara went so far as to design his own line of clothing and accessories, based around what was worn in the manga for women to buy. Shōjo manga has continued this type of illustration into contemporary books: *Sailor Moon* characters absolutely strut their looks straight off the catwalk, and it is still very popular to try and recreate the looks shown on characters by cosplayers and non-cosplayers alike. However, it wasn't until the 1970s that cosplay began to get its feet under the tables of Japanese manga fans.

The first record of cosplay, or at least costumes of a sort, at a Japanese convention or comic market was in 1974, at Miyacon. In the handbook for the comic market is listed the "Yoskio Aramaki Costume Show". This wasn't a costume competition or masquerade that would be seen today, but more of a performance. It was a selection of costume skits, featuring an array of both Japanese manga characters and popular American comic characters, including Captain America!

This is a similar vibe to the early masquerades and performances of the American and European conventions (see *A Guide to Film and Television Cosplay*). There is no indication that the costumes were worn on the convention floor or as part of anything but this performance, but it is not long before costumed fans start to turn up in other places.

Three years later, in 1977, a girl, whose name seems to be lost to the mists of time, was spotted at Comiket dressed as the main character from popular manga *Umi no Triton*. Her costume gained her the attention of the crowd, but much like her name, any photographs or articles have not been found. Sadly, the only reports of this costume were word of mouth from convention goers and organisers.

Cosplays from Nekocon.

Coincidentally, the character of Triton that she was cosplaying, is very heavily involved in the beginnings of cosplay in Japan. The manga was popular to the extreme in manga fan clubs in high schools across the country, and in 1977, in the 20th anniversary edition of the Japanese Sci-Fi magazine, *Uchujin*, a photo appeared of a group of high schoolers dressed as characters from *Umi no Triton*; the very same year as the mystery cosplayer at Comiket. Another cosplayer dressed in a similar outfit was spotted at a comic market a year later.

A lot of Japanese cosplayers consider these moments as the first real cosplays in Japan, the ones that set the seeds of the cosplay revolution that was to come.

1980s - Modern Day

In 1984 Nobuyuki Takahashi, writer, producer and founder of Studio Hard, attended the 42nd World Con in Los Angeles. He was a university student at the time in love with all things pop culture, so he and his friends headed to what was then the most well known convention in the world. Like many pop culture fans, they already had an inkling of knowledge about costuming at events, having seen a few costumes at Japanese Comic Markets, but nothing prepared them for what World Con had to offer. This stood far apart from what they knew.

Takahashi was inspired. The masquerades and Hero-costumes that he saw set something alight in him, and upon his return to Japan, he just had to tell everyone what he'd seen. He wrote a piece in the *My Anime* zine, describing the costumes for the first time, using the word cosplay.

The terms that were being used in the American and European convention scenes were clunky and old fashioned, especially when translated into Japanese; Fan costuming, hero-play and masquerade all ended up sounding "too noble and old fashioned" (quoted from Brian Ashcraft's book 'Cosplay World' featuring an interview with Takahashi) and Takahashi wanted a word that matched up with the youthful new hobby. Blending together the terms that he'd come across at World Con Takahashi finally settled on the word cosplay; a perfect mix of the art of costume and playfulness of the activity.

The Cosplay Handbook.

By the time the next Comiket, the biggest Japanese convention, rolled around people had taken cosplay to their hearts. It had become a phenomenon. Pop culture fans from all over Japan attended in costume, signposting the change of how cosplay would be seen around the world.

Despite the word being created in the 80s, cosplay as a term didn't catch on outside of Japan until the late 90s and early 2000s but that didn't mean that the ripples of cosplay, and Japanese pop culture in general, weren't being felt outside of the country.

Japanese cosplayers started taking their creations to shows around the world bringing with them new levels ofcrafting, and ideas about how costumes should be celebrated. Some would wear multiple costumes in a day and have five or six changes over a convention weekend! It really impressed other fans and cosplayers, encouraging bigger, better and bolder costumes in competitions and on the convention floor. It also saw western fans cosplaying from Japanese media more and more; a true exchange of ideas.

Manga, anime and Japanese video games were also becoming popular in the wider world during the 80s, 90s and 00s. Western cosplayers dressing as their favourite magical girl, giant sword wielding hero or zombie killing cop became regulars of the

Cosplay in *My Anime* Zine.

Cosplays from Katsucon and Animazement 1980s and 1990s, dates unknown.

convention scene where *Star Trek* and *Doctor Who* had only been seen before. The development of video games in Japan, bringing the traditional types of storytelling from manga into the digital age proved to be more popular than anyone would have guessed with companies like Nintendo taking centre stage in this new era of story creation.

Games like *Dragon Quest, Final Fantasy* and *Pokemon* combined the new technology of gaming with the storytelling elements of manga. Though this started out as relatively primitive, manga and anime were created alongside games to add more story and lore to the larger franchise which helped capture the imagination of fans, particularly younger ones, all over the world. *Pokemon* in particular succeeded in this: the anime, card game, toys, films and more that accompanied the handheld video game swept the world. You couldn't move for Pikachu and friends in the 90s and 00s and the popularity has never faded.

Pokemon brought in the wave of love for anime and video games in a whole generation outside of Japan in a way that nothing else had. Before this, manga, anime and gaming were a niche interest. Nerd culture was out of fashion, and those who were interested tended to stick with the European and American content, but the cute little electric mouse changed that. People started cosplaying as the characters and the Pokemon themselves without even knowing that's what they were doing, kids were dressing up as the cute pocket monsters for Halloween, and people could buy the clothing that was worn in the show. Japanese pop culture was here to stay, on a global scale.

Off the back of this, manga publishers in Europe and America, such as TokyoPop in the UK, started running small local events in bookshops and libraries to encourage more young people to start reading manga. They included cosplay as a large feature of these events with competitions and prizes for best cosplay and sometimes even invited experienced cosplayers to give talks on the subject for newcomers. For a lot of young people this was the first chance they got to see manga books properly, learn more about them and where they came from.

In Japan cosplay was everywhere. And not just at conventions. Cosplay cafes started popping up in Tokyo, staffed by servers dressed as peoples favourite characters, but cosplayers wanted more. There was a need for something bigger.

In 2003 the inaugural World Cosplay Summit was held in the city of Nagoya. Envisioned as a way to showcase and promote cosplay in Japan to the world, and vice versa, the World Cosplay Summit has become the centre of cosplay excellence. The international competition has been compared to the Olympics, with competitors competing to represent their country in the multi-day finals in Japan. In the most recent final (2019), 40 countries competed to take home the title of Grand Champion.

The first World Cosplay Summit, however, was not quite yet on this scale with only five countries, other than Japan, attending. It wasn't even a competition at this point either, more of an international gathering with panels, events and mixers for the cosplayers to get to know each other. The next year eight countries came, and the Cosplay Parade was introduced as an element of the Summit, but it wasn't until a year later that it started to evolve into the biggest cosplay competition in the world.

In 2005 the Cosplay Championships themselves were officially included as part of the World Cosplay Summit and from then on more and more countries began to attend. Cosplayers wanted the honour of representing their country and pushing to be the best they could be, as well as to see what ideas were being thought up by the community elsewhere.

Cosplays from Nekocon, Katsucon and Animazement 1980s and 1990s dates unknown.

This page and overleaf: Books and Merchandise from 90s Anime Conventions.

Other international competitions started to pop up all through the 2000s and 2010s inspired by what the World Cosplay Summit had achieved; The European Cosplay Gathering, Euro Cosplay, The Global Cosplay Championships, The World Cosplay Masters and The International Cosplay League just to name a few. All of them encourage the same ideals as the World Cosplay Summit of creativity, community and friendly competition.

While cosplay has been and always will be an international hobby and subculture, what Japan and Japanese pop culture has brought to the table has pushed it from a small community into a phenomenon. The inspiration taken from traditional stories and woven into modern manga and anime has given cosplay and pop culture in general, a unique style that would not have been there without it.

Where Do I Start?

Starting off on your cosplay journey is thrilling. Whether it's your first time getting involved in this amazing hobby, or you are side stepping into it from another costuming interest, or coming back to it after a break, there are a whole load of brilliant experiences awaiting you. Cosplay is not a fixed thing; like any art form there are so many aspects to draw from and be inspired by. You can start in one place and finish somewhere entirely different and never match up with anyone else's method. Sometimes you'll cross paths and match up with ideas, styles and projects but for the most part it's your thing and you're doing it your way. The joy of this is that you can make whatever you want.

People cosplay from everything and anything: films, TV shows, video games, anime, comics, manga and cartoons, books, music videos, podcasts, live streams and tabletop roleplaying games (or RPGs). The sky is most certainly the limit. You can replicate whether you want to replicate perfect versions of an on-screen costume, or completely make it up from your own idea of what your favourite book character looks like, or experiment with everything in between.

The range of choice can be a dream but having this wide and varied scope of things may feel daunting to start with – but don't panic. Find what you want to cosplay and focus on that. This may, and probably will, change as you cosplay for longer but don't let yourself feel pressured to do what's 'cool' or 'popular' if you don't like them. You may be the only person who knows what it is, but if you love it enough to want to be a character from it, then do it!

There can be this idea that cosplaying from manga, anime and video games is something that is less popular at European or American events nowadays, being more common in Japan, but this just simply isn't true. Some of the most popular characters to cosplay all over the world are from these media – after all, look at Mario or Sailor Moon! Disney, and all that comes with it, hasn't quite managed to take over the cosplay world just yet.

Lots of conventions around the world specialise in manga, anime and gaming and many of the big comic cons have sections dedicated to them. You're not going to be the only person picking a character that's not from a film or TV show.

A GUIDE TO MANGA, ANIME AND VIDEO GAME COSPLAY

If you're struggling with how to pick a character, get started with your cosplay, and the hows, whys and whats of creating screen-accurate costumes, then *A Guide to Movie and TV Cosplay*, the twin of this book, has got you covered. In this volume, however, we will be looking into more of the detail of bringing your favourite character out of the pages of manga and into real life.

When it comes to costumes from anime, manga and video games, aiming for a 'perfect' replica is probably not going to be possible (though of course there are exceptions to any rule). If there is artistic stylisation of the characters that doesn't translate across into reality, replicating it outside of a book can be especially tricky. But that's OK. Honestly, it's a great challenge. Think about it this way: the costume you want to make never existed in reality so you have free reign over how you are going to bring it into existence. You're bringing something brand new into the world and that's

Nott the Brave –
*Critical Role
Campaign Two.*

pretty magical. Even if someone has made the same character before, it's never going to be quite the same as your version. That's special to you. Add to this the mass influx of people cosplaying their own designs and creation, and you can see an ocean of possible design aesthetics and ideas for you to dive right into.

Cosplaying as your *Dungeons and Dragons* (or tabletop RPG of your choice) character has taken the cosplay scene by storm in the last few years, as has cosplaying from books and podcasts, where people are making up their own designs for characters based on descriptions and personal preference. These original designs are encouraging cosplayers from every 'genre' of cosplay to try their hand at some new creative processes when it comes to costume design. All of this leads to a whole load of exciting thinking skills and design processes that are very different, but equally as useful to a costume maker, as those you would use when creating a replica piece.

But we are getting ahead of ourselves. Why don't we take a look at bringing 2-D characters out of the manga and into our cosplay wardrobe, before we venture into the Narnia of original design.

Moving from Fiction to Reality

Cosplaying as a character from a comic or animation or game is very common. Lots of people like spending a day at Comic Con feeling as if they are in their favourite anime and there are plenty of different elements of bringing a character to life that need to be considered. Moving from what are basically flat images to a costume that you can interact with needs some thinking about. Costumes in manga, anime, cartoons, video games, and comics don't need to work in the real world so it's up to you how these 2-D designs, or 3-D models, can be translated into reality. Cartoony or realistic, straight off the page or adding your own twist, the sky really is the limit as long as you can figure out how.

Working with designs massively differs from three-dimensional media like films, TV or theatre. You won't have the same level of detail that exists in references of something that exists in reality. Nor the stability of it looking one, certain way throughout the show or film. Any item or garment in film, TV or theatre will have continuity in a way that animated or drawn mediums don't have. Mediums like cartoons and anime, comics and manga will often have different artists working on different issues, episodes, or series, so a design that is unchanged throughout an entire series can look different from book to book, episode to episode or even panel to panel. If you think that's frustrating, sometimes the same character will look different when they are shown in a different medium. Nightmare!

For example, in a manga the design for a character may look one way because it has to be drawn many times, often in motion, but in a piece of official art it may look more complex and detailed since this is in a one-off image. Then if it has an anime to go with it, as many manga do, the outfit may be different again to allow for ease of animation or because the animator(s) have a somewhat different drawing style to the original artist. So not only do you have variation within the different artists but also due to the stylisation of different media.

And talking of stylisation, many artists will have a style of drawing that doesn't translate to an obvious real-life analogue at all. This could be to be with the complexity of the design; large, complex shapes that defy the laws of physics or materials and fabrics behaving in a way they just don't (see almost any character wearing a bodysuit), or it could be as simple as the way they have coloured the characters hair or the fabrics they are wearing.

A perfect example of stylisation is a character like Sailor Moon. Is her hair blonde? Or is it actually bright yellow? In the visuals it's clearly yellow but is that a stylistic choice by the artist to represent that this character is blonde or a larger-than-life character whose hair is literally yellow? In some promotional art and art outside of the manga or anime her hair is coloured blonde, sometimes it has different tones in it – there's no clear answer. That means it is up to you as the cosplayer to decide for yourself.

Above and opposite:
Victor and Yuri –
Yuri!!!.

This can be annoying when you are trying to work out how to bring it to life, sure, but it can also give you room to play around. When it comes to characters with fluctuating designs like this you simply aren't going to be able to be 'accurate' in your creation, you can just do what you think looks good based on your own research. Is it a plaid skirt or is that the shadow of the pleats making it look like that? Is the armour white with black/grey details or is that just grooves in the armour being depicted by line work? You pick. Do what you think will look best in your style as a creator.

You have to remember that you as a cosplayer, are as much an artist as the person who did the drawing in the first place. You have a style all your own just as much as they do. Whether you realise it or not, as a cosplayer you will probably develop something in your work that is very distinctly you. You could have certain things that you always do in your sewing even if it's not in the original design (I will hold my hands up to excessive topstitching on everything), or a distinct way you sculpt your pieces, or the way you paint. But what all of this rolled up together means is that if you think a piece in a costume should look a certain way, that's fine. You do you. It'll look amazing because it's how you wanted it to be.

Let's Get Original

Ok, let's talk about redesigns and original designs.

A lot of cosplayers are looking to expand their creative talents, and with tabletop role playing games becoming popular again, *Dungeons and Dragons*, *Call of Cthulhu*, *Vampire: The Masquerade* and *Quest* being a few of the big ones, as well as more people crossing over between different types of costuming, this has provided the perfect excuse to head on down the designing rabbit hole. You can also see the influence of drag artists and LARPers who are either having a go at cosplay themselves or bumping up against the cosplay world in other ways, sprinkling their ways of creating costume designs over the cosplay scene.

Crossover costumes like Disney Princess Jedi, Harley Quinn Warhammer or Deadpool and, well, anything you can think of, have become very popular as people want to stand out from the crowd with expressive new designs. This has coincided with a trend for redesigning things like Pokémon, or other more animal-like characters, into human forms. These designs have drawn from huge amounts of different art styles and cultures, widening the net of character representation beyond what it had been in the past.

Some artists have even become famous for their work redesigning characters for cosplay. Hannah Alexander and Sunset Dragon are both very well-known within the global cosplay community for their sleek redesigns. Hannah Alexander focuses on the art nouveau style, with beautiful flowing designs reflective of the characters' original look and the series they are from, while Sunset Dragon creates stunning evening and ball gown designs, drawing from vintage and catwalk fashion. Many cosplayers have recreated their designs or have been inspired by them to do their own takes in this way.

One of the biggest areas of inspiration to recently appear in the cosplay scene is that of podcasts and streamed tabletop roleplaying games. These shows have encouraged a lot of cosplayers into designing, due to the desire to cosplay characters that exist almost exclusively using oral story telling methods. With possibly one or two images and descriptions included in the shows, many cosplayers have taken to dreaming up their own ideas of these characters. This is often done through collaborative methods across fandom pages, Discord chats, and social media, with them coming up with mutual ideas of the characters, but this doesn't stop someone listening to the show for the first time thinking up their own imagery for the characters in question. The new concepts and costumes that spring from this source have pushed people to widen their ideas of where cosplay can come from and what it can be, encouraging them to start looking more at audio drama, podcasts and the like for character inspiration. Once you've got the bug for this type of cosplay it's hard to go back. Interestingly this has also led to cosplayers turning to a less modern medium: books.

Below and opposite: Rincewind and Twoflower – Terry Pratchett's Discworld.

Cosplaying from books is far from new, but it is definitely having a resurgence. The gain in popularity of young adult fiction, particularly fantasy and sci-fi novels, and a fair amount of film or TV adaptions of these books not living up to fandom's ideas, has given rise to people taking the characters they love into their own hands and creating their own versions.

Like podcast cosplaying, there may well be some illustrations accompanying any given novel, and of course there will be character description in the text, but books are so subjective the cosplays that are born from them enter a whole new world of design. No one costume will be the same as another, but they will all be recognisable as the character to other fans. It is a very cool thing to have the same base idea for a character reflected through different people's personal vision and come out in a kaleidoscope of different interpretations. Plus the excitement of being able to talk about the way you have constructed an image from something in the text to other fans, and then comparing your thoughts, 'headcanons' and theories is definitely one of the best things about any form of cosplay. But especially these ones.

All of this eventually leads you into original design costumes of completely original characters.

While original design was one of the biggest elements of the first cosplays back in the

1930s/40s, and has been a long-standing part of LARP, Steampunk and other costuming hobbies, it has been out of fashion in cosplay for several decades. But there has been a mass resurgence in the last couple of years. This is in no small part due to the previously mentioned resurfacing popularity of tabletop role playing games, but also to apps like TikTok, where LARPers and cosplayers have started to combine their hobbies and bring about their own stories through episodic online LARPs. Cosplaying as your own invention is incredibly freeing and allows those who might not be able to afford to start cosplaying or have been worried about starting for whatever reason a space where they can experiment, create, and play without having to worry about being perfect. It also allows more experienced cosplayers a place to have fun, flex those crafting muscles and do new things with their skills.

The more options the hobby has, the more fun it's going to be. It's all about play, and it's important to remember that play is not just the physical acting side of cosplay, but experimentation, creative expression, developing of new skills, and building new connections and friendships through shared ideas and experiences.

Got all that? Good, because it's time to get on with actually breaking down designs and creating a costume, because you can't make any type of cosplay if you don't know where your starting point is.

Percival De Rollo and Vex'ahlia – *Critical Role Campaign One.*

What's in the Design?

Just a small note before we start: if you're thinking 'is this section more about redesign and original design costumes?' and you aren't interested that, remember all of these skills can be applied when you're thinking about bringing manga, anime, and comics characters to life too. In much the same way that you may not use resin casting or embroidery in every project but they are definitely going to be used on something, knowing about design and different types of design process will help inform everything you do as a creator.

Whether you are working from an existing design, redesigning one or making your own character, taking time to research, draw and perfect your ideas will make all the difference. This will allow you to see the design every which way before you being to fabricate anything. It will help you think about how the layers of garments or armour will fit together, give you a place where you can note down fabric and material ideas as well as get a feel for how the different materials will work together, and generally find all those little tweaks and changes you need to make before you start crafting.

The Ankh-Morpork City Watch – *Terry Pratchett's Discworld.*

And no, you do not need to be good at drawing. As long as you can get the basic ideas down on paper and you write notes next to it, you're golden. After all only you need to understand it.

Even professional designers aren't always the most amazing of artists (check out some of the original *Star Wars* designs for example). There is always the option of downloading 'fashion model templates' from the internet and use those to sketch your ideas on. You can find them in all sorts of shapes and sizes to help you create your vision on the page.

In *A Guide to Movie and TV Cosplay* we talked about collecting reference images, but with characters from 2-D mediums like manga and anime and redesigns or original designs this process can be slightly different.

Research

Princess Hilda –
Legend of Zelda: A Link Between Worlds.

Researching a character is one of the most important things to do before starting any cosplay project. Whether you are making or buying or a bit of both, you want to know what that character looks like inside outside, upside down and back to front. Every angle, every close up, every layer of clothing or armour if you can find it. Try and get your hands on as many different images, GIFs, and videos as you can to help grow your knowledge. Building up your reference images will put you in a good place going forward but you may need to go further. You'll get to a point where you know this costume inside out, but you should still go that little bit further just to be sure. You don't want to find you've missed something important.

Working on a character who only exists in 2-D manga, comics, or anime often means that the fabrics and the materials that make up their outfits don't move or sit in the way that they would in real life. A cloak or skirt may look like it's floating or blowing effortlessly behind the character, something that could be achieved with a very light weight fabric like chiffon, but the way it hangs the rest of the time or its use in the context of the story shows that it should be heavy fabric. Garments like warm winter cloaks or large circle skirts are often the worst for this since the design is unlikely to have a fabric depicted beyond a few lines; you as the costume

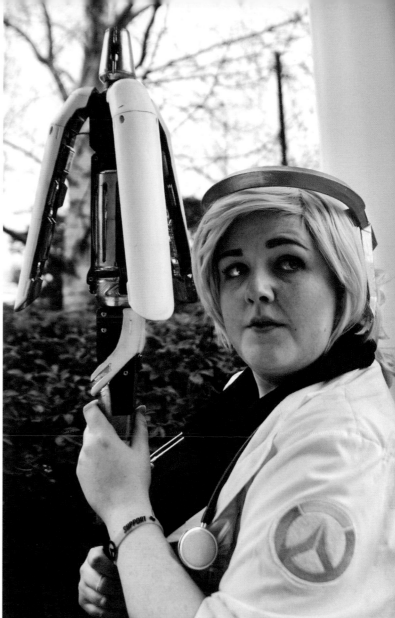

Mercy – *Overwatch.*

maker will have to make a judgement on what fabric you want to use to bring this garment into reality.

Researching fabrics and materials is always a large part of any costume build, but when it comes to 2-D designs you may find yourself going into a rabbit hole of what will work. Whether you are making your own, commissioning from another cosplayer or even buying 'off the shelf' it's worth having an understanding of the materials that are going to be used either by you or the person constructing the costume for you. Make sure that you get samples of all the fabrics you think will work, and all the materials – such as foams, leathers, plastics, and others – you want to make your costume from. If you are doing any type of painting, swatch any new paints that you are going to use to get an idea if they are exactly what you want. This will not only help you on the costume build you are currently focused on, but build up your overall knowledge as an artist.

Having a little folder of your collected research is no bad thing at all. Being able to flip through what you've used before rather than rummaging through your boxes of

Right and opposite: Dante – Devil May Cry 5.

leftover materials or having to remember what you did last time is so helpful. It will make it easier to make the decisions about how you want to bring that strange floaty cloak to life; especially when you inevitably end up with the same problem with another costume in the future.

Another large part of your research can be looking at fashions, costumes and garments that are similar to your character's design. This ties into choosing your fabrics and materials by giving you an idea of how pieces like this have been made before.

Looking at historical and vintage clothing, modern fashion designers and other cosplayers/costume makers will give you great ideas of how to put your own costume together. They can also help you think about the aesthetic look you want to create. Do you want to go hyper-realistic or super cartoony, in between, or something completely off-piste? Your design will inform your fabric choices and your research will inform your design. At no point is learning from others a bad thing, and it will definitely save you from a few obvious mistakes along the way.

As for where to do your research, you cannot have too many sources. Outside of the source material itself, books, magazines, Pinterest, Instagram, online reference libraries, fashion shows, historical and fashion documentaries, even shows like *The Great British Sewing Bee,* can all be sources for research and inspiration.

If you're looking at creating garments from other cultures, for example Japanese

cultural costume appears in a lot of manga and anime, research into that as well. The historical and cultural meaning behind garments is something that you should be aware and respectful of in your creation. Understanding how to show appreciation instead of appropriation of cultural elements when cosplaying as a character that has elements of cultural dress involved in their design is a must, so build this into your research.

Design Process

Designing is a skill in cosplay that has blossomed as the hobby has expanded, and is continuing to do so. While original design work has been used for years, since cosplay first started, with fashion catwalks inspired by science fiction being a major draw of early conventions, there has been a tendency over the last couple of decades to shy away from designing your own costumes, with more emphasis being put on recreating existing ideas. But no longer. Cosplayers have very clearly made a move to celebrate their own creativity and are excited to showcase their original work once again.

A lot of cosplayers have turned to professional designers from different backgrounds. This is a great way to start getting a feel for designing as both a craft (sketching up and getting the design on paper) and an art (imagining and envisioning the design in the first place).

Professional costume designers will spend a long time thinking through the characters, looking over scripts, and getting a general overview of who this person is, whose visual appearance they are literally creating from scratch. And cosplayers do this too.

If you are interested in designing, track down advice from professional designers. There are some great books, interviews, courses and the like out there to learn from people in the industry. While, of course, there aren't the same 'rules' as a film production or a stage show with cosplay – cosplayers can make whatever they want, however they want, it's their hobby – taking some tips from the professionals to add to your arsenal of skills is no bad thing.

But for now let's take a look at some easy ways of starting designing for yourself.

There are a couple of different ways you can approach your design process when making your cosplay. For the sake of this section, we are going to call them Character Focused and Aesthetic Focused:

- Character Focused is looking at the character, their personality, their environment, their job, how they fit into the story, and how that is reflected in their appearance.
- Aesthetic Focused is looking at creating a different aesthetically pleasing or interesting version of the character. This could be based on fashion styles (e.g. Lolita, Steampunk or ballgowns), crossing them over with another universe/story (e.g. Jedi Pokémon or Sailor Scout Disney Princesses), or simply wanting to go to town with your ideas.

You could see it basically as the difference between designing for film/theatre/TV/etc, versus designing for fashion.

Straw Ops – *Fortnite.*

Character Focused

With Character Focused design the best place to start is by asking yourself three questions: Where do they come from? What do they do? What are their character traits?

These are quite broad questions but they can help you pinpoint a lot of information about a character. If you think of a character now, it doesn't need to be one that you want to design for, just one that you can use as an example for yourself. Let's go through those questions to understand how they can help.

Where do they come from?

The answer to this could be the series, film or game they are from, for example Luke Skywalker is from *Star Wars*. However, this answer could also be where are they from within the story, so Luke is from the desert planet, Tatooine. But he's also from a small farm in the deserts of Tatooine.

Luke Skywalker –
Star Wars: Return of the Jedi.

All of these answers are helpful when thinking about the character and will have been applied by the costume designer for the film. He's in *Star Wars* so there is an overall type of design that was used in the films to give the universe a characteristic aesthetic. Then layering that he is from a certain planet, Tatooine, means that he will dress in a certain way because of the fashions of that planet/area. Also knowing that he is from a small farm outside of the towns/cities says that he is probably going to be a little more rough and tumble, probably not that up with fashions and generally more workaday in his appearance.

So, if you are doing your own character design, say of Luke as if he were from Naboo, his mother's home planet, you would go and look at the designs that are used on Naboo and apply those instead of designs from Tatooine. Since his mother was queen and is a senator, you would look at Padme and the other high-powered senators and leaders for the types of fashion they wear instead of the clothes of a worker. You might even make him a prince, but you would keep the overall *Star Wars* aesthetic to the design.

You can apply this to any redesign or original design. Ask yourself where they are from and build up a picture of the aesthetics of that media and the locations within it to inform your ideas.

What do they do?

Again, with this question there are multiple answers that can add up to a bigger picture of what the design needs, requires or wants to have for it to work how you want.

This could be what do they do for a job, such as being a soldier, or a baker, or an adventurer; but it could also be what they do within the story, and the role they play in the telling of the story and as a character. Or what do they physically do, e.g. do they run and climb and jump around all the time, or are they more the type to sit in an armchair and observe the world around them.

If we go back to Mr Skywalker, Luke is a Jedi and a pilot, so knowing what people in those jobs look like and wear as a uniform or similar will be helpful to know. But his role as a Jedi, what he's doing in the story, changes from novice to master over the course of the films and so does his wardrobe; from white in the first film to black in the last. But he also runs around a lot and needs to be mobile, which means that his clothes reflect that, until the last film where he is much more confident in his abilities, and his appearance reflects that by becoming more tailored and controlled.

In a redesign, let's use the Naboo Prince Luke concept again. You could look at how the senators and royalty of Naboo behave and what they do within the story. His mother, Padme, is a perfect example as she does not tend to be the running, jumping type, mostly being seen as politician, and dressing accordingly. Though not always (white jumpsuit anyone?). So in this role Luke would be more likely to be dressed in the somewhat over the top fashions that lack practicality as he is not required to be practical.

That leads us to the last question…

What are their character traits?

This one is a little bit easier. What is the character like? Are they cute and bubbly or grumpy and stubborn, do they have a mix of traits depending on who they are with or how they are feeling? Are they innocent and naïve in their outlook or jaded by the horrors they have witnessed? When it comes to designing, a character's personality affects how they dress as much as their environment does. In the same way that you pick the clothes you wear for a reason, so does a character.

A bubbly, cute, or younger character's traits might be reflected in more 'childish' design: bright colours, large prints or patterns on the clothes, cute shorts or frilly dresses, scraped knees, etc.

A dark, brooding, adult character is more likely to appear with more subdued design: dark colours, subtle design or no prints or embellishments at all unless it's 'practical'; garments that cover the body to 'hide' in.

Luke Skywalker – *Star Wars: Return of the Jedi.*

This could go even deeper into their traits as well. Your character could be a very optimistic person but having to hide who they are physically or emotionally, so that might be something you want to reflect in the design by mixing different visuals together. They may look like a brooding villain but have an item on them that shows something of the inner self. It's fun to play around with.

Once again Luke is a perfect example of character traits reflected in costume. In the first film he is young, optimistic but naïve, looking for something beyond himself so his clothes are white, with simple garment design and loose fitting. This shows that he is young and innocent. They are much more representative of the clothing of a teenager who doesn't know that much about the world around him, than those worn by Han, who is older and more careworn, or those of Leia, who whilst young is more mature and has less naïvety of the world.

We understand a huge amount about him as a person from his appearance, and all these little visual signals click into the viewer's brain and explain elements of the character without having to express it in dialogue. But it is worth thinking about which point in the character's story you are looking at when asking this question.

As stated before, when Luke has 'grown-up' in the third film, his entire appearance has changed to more adult garments that are more like those that have been shown before on older, more mature characters. He is wearing darker colours to show the loss of his innocence, so the viewer can see that he has learnt lessons and understanding that he lacked before, not just through his actions but through his presence and appearance. His character traits have changed and his design has changed with them.

Looking at the redesign idea, Prince of Naboo Luke may appear as a more happy-go-lucky character to you because he hasn't had the same troubles of the events in the films. This could lead to more outlandish, colourful designs to show his *laissez-faire* attitudes. Or it could be that he is more like Leia, a cunning politician and rebel leader, so his appearance would be more in line with her simple yet classic appearance, showing that she is both a leader and rebellious in her nature but knows how to play the role of princess.

Asking these three questions will inform your research, since you will have more of an idea what you are looking for and will give you a better starting point for your design. The more information you can give yourself about the character you are designing for, the more you will be able to build the visual appearance of this character to feel in tune with them as a character and the world they inhabit.

You can apply these questions to any character, it doesn't have to be one that comes from a series with a large number of pre-existing designs and aesthetic to work from. You can even use these questions on characters from books, podcasts, and media that have no visual representation; it works just as well. Looking for descriptions in the text or from other characters talking about the character can give you clues, as well as things like their actions and characteristics. And your ideas don't have to match up with other people's, this is your interpretation, so it is what you read in the text and what you get from the character that give you the answers to the questions. Art is completely subjective after all.

Granny Weatherwax,
Nanny Ogg and
Magrat Garlick –
*Terry Pratchett's
Discworld.*

Aesthetic Focused

On the flip side of this is Aesthetic Focused design. Think of this more of fashion design being born out of a wish to create a stylised version of a character or an outfit inspired by them. This type of design is more likely to see things like Steampunk or Lolita redesigned versions of a character, or similar ideas as you place an aesthetic onto a character design.

When you are doing designs like this, part of your idea building should be looking into the limits of the aesthetic you want to use. In the same way that you ask questions of your character, ask questions of the aesthetic.

Sailor Moon, Princess Merida Crossover.

What defines this aesthetic?

Fashion and artistic aesthetics will be defined by certain traits. This is how you can tell that they are what they are. Art Deco is obviously different from Art Nouveau, with it having rigid lines and industrial shapes as opposed to Art Nouveau being organic curves and flowing lines. You can instantly tell the difference. What this means for design is that when you want to use an aesthetic for a project it is important you understand the key points that define it in order for your design to be seen as that aesthetic.

For example if you wanted to make a Lolita version of Sailor Moon then you should start with researching into Lolita fashion and what makes up that aesthetic. Lolita has rules that define it. In order for an outfit to be Lolita you must create the right dress silhouettes, have a skirt of a certain length or longer, have the correct styles of blouse, wear certain types of accessories and hair styles, and beyond. There are even guidelines on what types of print or patterns are used in each sub-style of Lolita. So taking a look at all of these things and finding out the whats, whys, and wherefores of the fashion will mean that you will be able to apply this to your Lolita Sailor Moon so it can be recognised as specifically Lolita inspired.

You can do this with every type of aesthetic. Sometimes there may be written 'rules' to define it, or it may be that you need to look at lots of examples of that aesthetic and note down the consistent things that you see, such as using

Sailor Moon, Princess Merida Crossover.

mechanisms and clockwork in Steampunk, or neon colours and chunky accessories in rave wear.

This is also something that you should do when doing a crossover cosplay. A crossover cosplay is a costume that combines two fandoms together. This is where you get your Sailor Scout Disney Princesses or Mandalorian Bakugou cosplays and the like.

Since you are combining the aesthetic of a uniform from one piece of media, for example the Sailor Scouts uniforms from *Sailor Moon*, with a character from another piece of media, say Merida from Disney Pixar's *Brave*, you need to know what defines the aesthetic of the uniform before you place the traits of the character onto it. In the same way that you would look at any other fashion or artistic aesthetic you would look at the aesthetics of the uniform design. The skirt style, the puffy sleeves, the sailor suit neckline and collar, the blocks of colour and how they are placed, and so on, then taking these recognisable elements to use in your design. In this case you could have the typical Sailor Scout skirt made from a fabric with the teal blue of Merida's dress, with a matching collar, boots and gloves in the same or a similar colour, and the white main body of the uniform could stay the same or you could change it to blue like the rest of the costume, as Merida does wear a dress in one block colour. Then it's all about adding details and important motifs of the character to draw the whole concept together. And don't forget those massive bows that Sailor Scouts are known for!

Once you have the knowledge of the aesthetic and understand what makes it work, designs will start popping straight into your head.

What are the character's visual and aesthetic traits?

This question is sort of the flip side of the coin to the first. Where before you needed to understand the fashion aesthetic you wanted to place onto a character, this question asks you to consider the visual elements of the character to make sure it is recognisable as that character.

Every character has an element of their design that is quintessentially them, that you could see from across a convention hall or in the background of a scene in an anime and know it's them. It could be certain colours in a certain pattern, it could be a logo or symbol that they always have as part of their costume, it could be how they do their hair or their braid, it could be an item that they always have on them, or it could be a mix of some or all of these things. That thing (or those things) is what you need to pinpoint in the character design/s you are working from and carry into your own version.

How are we going to know that your ballgown is based on Pikachu if it doesn't have the colours or markings of Pikachu? Even then that might not be enough to carry the idea of Pikachu onto the ballgown, so you might need to include the classic lightning bolt tail somehow, so that image of Pikachu flashes into the mind; maybe this could be as a train on the skirt. You might include pokeball hair corsage or clutch bag, or you could also include Pikachu or Pokémon themed jewellery.

All these elements of Pikachu-ness added to the ballgown make it obvious who the design is based on, shouting 'HEY! I'm Pikachu!' whilst not losing the aesthetic of the fashion.

Try to keep it relatively simple and obvious. If you are making a Pikachu ballgown, then the gown is going to be the complex part of the image you are portraying. Overwhelming it with lots of little bits and pieces muddies what you are trying to

Below and overleaf:
Hanayo Koizumi –
Love Live.

create. So pick those obvious elements. The colours, the tail, the pokeball. Use them sparingly and where needed to let the whole thing shine with the two combined ideas.

You can also reverse engineer any of these questions from either type of design process when looking at an existing design you want to make, asking why certain choices have been made for this design and what that tells you about the character. Having some idea of these things can be incredibly helpful when you are making that costume and in the decisions you make about the build.

But these are just some ideas for designing and redesigning characters; you can go completely out there and do something that inspires you instead.

Refine your Design

This stage is the easiest to explain. Keep working on your design until you are completely happy. Go over it as much as you want to work out all the little kinks and flaws in the look of the thing and the build process until you think you have it right.

All that research, thinking and processing that you have done will feed subconsciously into your designs. And don't stop doing those things just because you are drawing the design out; let your work be informed by what you are finding out. You may hit a problem as you're refining your concept or moving into the build process, such as how to make a gauntlet. So go back to your research and see if you have looked that up already, and if not, it's now a new little piece of research to do that you can add to your skills. Don't know what a certain item of clothing should look like as you're sketching? Think over the questions you asked yourself about the design to see if something about the character can help you figure that out.

The whole thing is organic.

Don't be afraid of doing three, four, five, ten sketches, maybe even more. Trying out different concepts, and even throwing in things you maybe don't think will work, can change the way you are looking at the project. It gives you perspective.

The whole point of design work is that it is a process. It's part of the build, not separate from it. You don't need to push for design number one to be a perfect masterpiece straight off the bat. All of that thinking, researching and processing that you have done needs time to settle and combine in both your mind and on the paper.

It's also important to remember that your sketches aren't the final design. The final version is the version you wear and even then you may never stop tweaking it. You can always be adding, changing and modifying your ideas no matter what part of the build you are in. If you find yourself doing this, whether you are playing with a bit of the design or modifying a pattern you're using, make a note of it in your research folder or in your phone or wherever you keep track of your progress, so you know for the future. Sometimes you might even find you want to change your costume after you've worn it, and that's totally fine too.

However you go about this process, remember that it's your costume. Have fun with it – that's the most important part.

SECTION 3

Making Cosplay and What Happens Next

Sally Face – *Sally Face*.

There is no single skill or skill set that defines cosplay. When you look at the credits list for a film you will see more roles and names than you would think possible working in each area to bring the story to the big screen, and a cosplayer in their time is likely to fill every one of those roles. On a professional level you need people who are an expert in one area to focus on that single area, but as a single person making costumes for their own enjoyment, or other personal reasons, you need to be a jack of all trades. While some people will have a particular skill set that they favour, foam armour work for example, they will still need to have an understanding of sewing, wig styling, props making, and a hundred other things to make and finish a costume.

You will also find that not only are you learning and practising the skills for making a costume, but you'll end up learning how to be a model so you can pose well, how to take photos so you can show off your costumes on social media and maybe even how to make videos and short films so you can tell your own little stories or showcase more elements of your costume. You end up as a one-person film crew without realising! And that can lead down all sorts of avenues of creativity.

But we're getting ahead of ourselves. Got to walk before you can run, so let's take a look at some of the skills you'll need to make your costume.

For sewing, armour and modifying costumes see *A Guide to Film and TV Cosplay*.

Wigs, and Make-up: Get the Full Look

One of the things that a lot of people find daunting when starting out cosplaying is wigs and make-up. While we are very used to styling our own hair and possibly doing a daily make-up routine, there is a difference between doing that and creating the perfectly styled wig and performing a full make-up transformation on our own faces to look more like a character. It's a bit of challenge to learn how to get to grips with these new skills and refine them.

But don't be too worried or overwhelmed. There is a lot of great help out there for even the trickiest of wigs and make-up looks, with tutorials that can teach you everything need to know, from a natural look all the way up to full drag-inspired creations.

Angua Von Uberwald and Cheery Littlebottom – *Terry Pratchett's Discworld.*

Wigs

First off, you don't always need a wig for a costume. If your natural hair looks good for that character then go for it, and wigs aren't for everyone. You are not less of a cosplayer for not using wigs all the time. However, there are going to be times when having a pre-styled wig will just make the costume pop and your life that little bit easier on the day of the convention. It's not easy to do Super Saiyan hair in real life.

There are two basic types of wig that cosplayers use: the standard and the lace front. You can get other types, such as a full lace wig, but these are, in general, a lot more expensive.

The standard wig is normally a good base for styling and adding more hair or hair pieces to (like clip-on ponytails) and they all have full fringes as they do not have a natural hair line. This type of wig is great for cosplaying any character with heavy bangs or a stylised fringe. They come in loads of colours and are perfect for more 'cartoon' styles and characters.

Lace fronts are more natural looking, with a realistic hair line so you don't need a fringe. These can be heavily styled into almost anything, but there doesn't tend to be the same range of colours available unless you are willing to spend more. This is changing though, so always keep an eye out for new colours of lace front popping up. Lace fronts are often used by drag queens and in theatre because of their more natural look.

Fiona – *Tales from the Borderlands.*

You can also get add-ons and accessories for wigs such as wefts, the single strands of hair that make up a wig, very similar to a clip-in hair extension; clip- or sew-in hair pieces including ponytails, braids, buns and more; for non-human characters you may well want to have horns or animal ears of some sort coming out of a wig which you can buy or make.

Both types of wigs have a myriad of uses and just as many tutorials across YouTube, cosplay forums, Facebook groups and books (check the References section for some recommendations). You will also be able to find more information about wigs in general and other types of wigs there too.

A lot of manga, anime and video game characters have hair that is a bit out of this world, defying gravity with spikes, curls, flicks and fringes heading out into the atmosphere, so having a constructed, pre-styled wig that you know is going to hold its own all day will make your life easier.

For a lot of wigs like this, they aren't even all hair. Often they will have foam structures with synthetic hair glued onto the outside and blended to create the appearance of a great mass of hair. It's a lot lighter, cheaper and easier to control as a build. It may be that the whole wig base is made from foam, including the cap (so it's more like a helmet) and then has the hair added onto the shape.

Sometimes people want super cartoon wigs and use this technique, but instead of using hair they add strips of foam to look like hair and paint it. It is very effective for highly stylised characters. The characters from the *Borderlands* game franchise are perfect examples of stylisation that this could be used for.

You can also do these wig styles with multiple wigs sewn together to give more body, or extra wefts that can be sewn into the wig cap if you don't want to do a foam build. Back combing, steaming and lots of hairspray, sometimes even glue, can achieve this look as well. It can work great if you want to create a more 'realistic' version of these dramatic styles rather than a cartoony one, so it's up to your personal preference.

For more natural or realistic look overall with a wig you are going to want to stick with the more traditional hair-based styling methods. Great places to start with on how to style natural looking or lace front wigs are the drag community and hair stylists of the black community, where wig wearing is more common. Both of these groups have a huge amount of expertise on how to DIY wigs, style them and make them from scratch, as well as how to keep them on all day without having to worry – the most useful piece

Fiona – *Tales from the Borderlands.*

of advice for a long day at a convention. Just because you're a cosplayer, doesn't mean you only have to learn from other cosplayers.

For buying wigs, you can go cheap as chips or you can be calling your bank for a loan; there's a huge range of choices. Some of the best are:

- Lushwigs
- Wig is Fashion UK
- Kyrssma
- CosCraft
- Arda Wigs

Toph Beifong – *Avatar: The Last Airbender.*

All of these are good quality and aren't going to bankrupt you. They do range in price depending on style, wig type, colour and length.

If you want to spend less and are willing to take a risk, you can get some amazing quality wigs on eBay and Amazon but it's often hard to tell, so check the reviews and see if other cosplayers have bought from them in the past. Lace front wigs are normally more expensive because of the hair line, but if that's what you need it's worth spending that little bit more on them.

There is as much experimentation and playing around to be done with wigs as there is in any other area of cosplay, so if you want to take it further there are ways to do it. Some cosplayers make their wigs from scratch, using hand knotting techniques (literally tying each strand of hair individually onto a lace wig cap or lace front wig – this can also be used for making facial hair pieces like beards) or sewing wefts onto a cap, to get exactly the look that they want. If you aren't quite up to that you can modify an existing wig by adding extra wefts to add more colour variation, or change the wig's texture or shape. Others may go to extremes with modification by putting things like LEDs and miniature smoke machines into their wigs, making them look as if they're on fire or changing through a colour spectrum. Definitely a show stopper!

It really is amazing what you can do with a wig.

Make-Up

Make-up is a part of cosplay that sometimes gets overlooked when you start out. Unless it's very obvious prosthetics, wounds and scars, or painting yourself blue, you might not even think about make-up as part of a costume. You've got the costume on, that's the main bit, but it can help enhance the whole thing by adding an extra little something to your face as well. Using make-up to create a likeness of a character or just to make sure your face doesn't look sweaty in photos after you've been running around a convention, can add a finished look to your costume.

Also it helps to know how to paint yourself blue if that moment arrives.

A lot of people wear make-up every day, which is a great starting place to build from, but if you don't know anything? That's OK too, because cosplay make-up isn't exactly the same as your day-to-day look. A lot of the time with make-up for a cosplay you are going to be working with a more extreme style or application; you don't want it coming off during the day because you've been sweating in a convention hall that lacks proper air-conditioning.

Knowing what make-up works for you, your face, your skin tone and type, will put you in good stead for trying more complex and dramatic techniques later. YouTube is a great starting point if you are a complete beginner, and you can always look up something new or find a new idea there even if you are a bit more confident with make-up. But where to even start? There are so many tutorials for so many different things!

Mollymauk Tealeaf – *Critical Role Campaign Two.*

Skin Tone and Type

One of the first things you are going to need to think about is your skin. Everyone's is different so what works for one person may not work for another, so have a think about your skin tone and your skin type.

Skin tone is the colour of your skin and the colours within that. You have the tone which will be light to dark, but you also have the undertone which can be generally categorised as cool, warm or neutral. People with cool skin tones tend to have more reds and blues in their skin, warm tones are more peach and yellow, and neutral is a blend of the two. Knowing which one of these you are will help you pick out foundation, concealer, blusher, and the contour and highlight tones that will work best for you.

Markus – *Detroit Become Human.*

There are a few different ways to work out your undertone. A good general starting place is to take a look at your eye colour. If you have brown or hazel eyes you are more likely to have a warmer or neutral undertone, with blue, green and grey eyes having a cool undertone. This isn't always the case but is a good starting point. To get a more accurate idea stand in an area with daylight, but not direct sunlight, and take a look at your wrist; specifically, your veins. If your veins are a bluey/purply colour you are more likely to have a cool undertone, and if they are greener then you are more likely to have a warm one. You may see both, which would suggest a neutral undertone. Artificial light won't give you an accurate colour balance as bulbs can have blue or yellow tones and trick the eye.

Once you know this you can look for products that match your skin tone and flatter your colouring.

You may also want to think about if your skin is dry or oily as this can also help you pick a better range of products that sit better on the face. Different skin types need looking after in different ways. For example, if you have dryer skin you may need more moisturising products as a base layer before using a foundation. And you can get more moisturising foundations and concealers as well if you think you need that. But if you have oily skin you will need to go the other way and look at base layers that help reduce oiliness and make the skin more matte before applying anything else.

There's a huge amount of information out there to help you, but if you get overwhelmed or you just don't know, a lot of make-up stores or counters will do a service to help you find your best match, and often you can book in for a full consultation or make-up class with them to learn first-hand from a make-up artist.

Masters of Disguise

Transforming yourself with make-up can mean a few different things. For some cosplayers there is an element of trying to make themselves look as much like a character as possible. This could mean aiming for 'look-a-like' transformation, using high levels of contour, highlight and 'sculpting' techniques to make yourself look like a character. For others its about embodying the character in their own way, so rather than transforming themselves to look like the character, they make the character look like them. They might use body paint to become an alien and a magical creature, and prosthetics to enhance or add to their face and skin. So many ways of doing things.

You will probably have seen a few cosplayers who specialise in perfecting the skills to transform themselves into exact doubles of characters. For the most part this type of make-up is used for film and TV characters where there is an actor to work from, or the more hyper-realistic looking animation in video games, but it's worth remembering that being a look-a-like is not the point of cosplay and you don't have to do this to be the character.

A lot of cosplayers will use make-up techniques to 'imply' the appearance of the character, recreating elements of the character's face and body that are important to their overall appearance. This could be adding prominent scars, tattoos or markings that appear on the character, or cuts and bruises that they acquire through the story.

For either of these types of character make-up, cosplayers will use contouring techniques to shape the face to create the impression of themselves as the character they are dressed as. It's one of the most used and useful make-up techniques around.

For anyone who doesn't quite understand what contouring is, it is adding the illusion of light and shadow on the face to sculpt it into a specific shape, either to exaggerate the shape you have or to change it to the shape you want. The darker shade will add depth and shadow to make those areas appear 'sunken' and the lighter/brighter colours will draw those areas of the face out more. For example, you would lighten the top of your cheek bone and darken underneath to make it pop. The more intense your tones the more extreme the look will become. It's good to practice and try different shades and how much you blend/don't blend out your contour to see what you want from a look.

Contouring can be done with a skin-toned contour palette, matte eyeshadows; or coloured eyeshadows and paints if you are doing a cosplay with body paint to make yourself look yellow, blue or some other fantastical skin colour.

Studying the face shape of who you are cosplaying or someone with a face shape similar to that you want to create will help you work out how you want to contour. Printing out a picture to mark the dark and light areas on their face might sound a little creepy but it will give you a great diagram of where to place the lighter and darker tones on your own face. Once you have the basic look you can then start adding details like scars, freckles, birthmarks, tattoos or any facial hair your character has on their face to build up the illusion.

Body and face paint cosplays are becoming a lot more common on the convention scene as well. Cosplayers who do these kinds of cosplays tend not to actually paint their whole body but instead use coloured tights and gloves made from sheer fabric, very similar to skin coloured tights, to give the impression of bright coloured skin whilst not having to worry about it coming off or everything they touch turning green. They then can paint their face and neck to match and the illusion is complete.

When it comes to make-up, the amount you use, the way you use it, or if you even wear it at all is personal preference. Having a base level of knowledge about using make-up can be helpful, but whether you use it or not does not make you any more or less valid as a cosplayer.

Add-Ons

If you want to cosplay as one of the many weird and wonderful magical characters out there you are going to need to get your hands on some prosthetics. These are additional pieces made from latex or silicone, such as ears and noses that you can attach, using a special skin-safe glue called spirit gum, to your face and body to make yourself look different. Elf ears are a very common sight at any convention or event, as are horns, facial ridges, and facial hair pieces, though that last one is a little different.

A lot of prosthetics are available online or in specialised theatre supply shops, and you can get them premade or commission a piece just for you. Premade is going to be cheaper and you can change, paint and modify the pieces as you need to fit your costume. A commission piece is definitely going up a price range, but if you need a

custom piece then this can be an option for you. You can also get commission pieces that are more realistic or better fitted to your features and skin tone as the maker will be working directly with you. Make sure that if you are going to use latex or theatre glues, you do a patch test on your skin first, as some people can be allergic and you don't want to end up in hospital after trying on your new elf ears.

This is also true of facial hair pieces. There are lots of different premade ones to pick from, but make sure you look at the quality of the one you are buying so it doesn't look fake. If you don't want to get a premade piece, a good and cheap option is crêpe hair, which you can buy in braids and glue layer by layer to your face to build up the facial hair you want, and then when it's dry you can trim it to shape.

You could always try your hand at making prosthetics yourself. Courses in theatre make-up and prosthetics are available, and there are some online tutorials and classes too, but be prepared to be spending more on learning this craft as the supplies are expensive, even if you are teaching yourself rather than paying for a course. However, classes will teach you more than just making a fake nose and moustache, so if this is an area you are interested in, look to see if you can find a course in your area.

Hank and Connor – *Detroit Become Human.*

Original Character – *Detroit Become Human.*

Props: Weapons, Puppets, and the Pound Shop, Oh My!

Something that cosplayers discover very early is that a prop can make all the difference to a costume. Having something to pose with for those convention floor snaps, act with in cosplay videos or use in photoshoots can just add a little extra dimension to a costume. While it's not always necessary to have a prop, and while some characters just don't have one or you may not want to be carrying something around all day, often having even a small prop can help bring the character to life.

Prop making can fall into the same category as armour making, but it definitely has its own place in the cosplay 'build canon' as it were. Many armour builders love making props, but that isn't always the case, and some people who love to make props do not like making armour. At all. The two things are not mutually exclusive, nor are they completely separate from sewers or wig and SFX specialists.

One of the joys of prop making is that you can just have a go and see what works. Not to undermine the incredibly skilled props makers working in both the community and professionally, but you can start out learning to build props pretty cheaply and easily with random odds and ends you can find in DIY stores, craft/hobby shops, or even just in your house, without having to get a load of specialised kit straight out of the gate.

All those Bits and Bobs

Did you know that Rey's staff in *Star Wars* is made out of pieces of plumbing piping and shower attachments? And that's in a film! So if you want to try your hand at props making, just go for it. Actually, all the *Star Wars* films have pieces that you wouldn't expect to be made from just household stuff (keep an eye out for pen lids next time you watch the prequel trilogy). And that's the same across a lot of films, TV shows, stage productions and even modelling 3-D pieces for games or animation. If it works, it works!

The amount of things you can find in the pound shop or in a charity shop that you can turn into something amazing is one of the true wonders of the cosplay world. Don't restrict yourself to the 'rules' of building in any area of cosplay, but especially not in props, because if the professionals are making it up as they go along because it looks cool, you can do that too! You can just play around and see what happens, and it won't break the bank.

You can literally start with something you just think looks right and go from there. You want a crystal ball? Cheap plastic fishbowl off eBay, some LED fairy lights from the pound shop and some holographic sticky back plastic from the craft store and you've got yourself something amazing for super cheap.

There are of course tutorials and tips online if you don't know where to start with something, which can be really helpful if you can't put your finger on the starting point for a piece, or what exactly that little thingamabob on the side of the blaster reminds you of. You don't have to do it all by yourself.

Make sure that you keep in mind that some materials will not be allowed at conventions due to safety rules, so check the convention's prop safety FAQ before you go. If they

Above and Opposite:
Soldier 76 –
Overwatch.

don't have any clearly listed try and contact them about it as it's not worth running the risk that all your hard work will be taken off you by security the moment you get there. Probably best not to use things like a 2 x 4 lump of wood and a load of nuts and bolts. Might not go down that well.

The good thing is that there are methods for making props out of convention-safe materials as well!

Light as a Feather

If you're worried that the prop you want to make might be or look dangerous you can try methods similar to the ones used for armour building. Foam, Worbla, 3-D printing and other armour making methods and materials are perfect for prop making too. And if you're not all that confident with large scale armour builds, props can be a great place to start to help build up those skills without the worry over cost.

Foam, 3-D printing and the like will also allow for lighter props, especially things like those oversized swords that do tend to turn up in manga, anime and video games (Cloud from *Final Fantasy VII* is a perfect example of this). Though Worbla may end up too heavy for large scale props, it can work very well for smaller ones and give more detail to something. You can also look at foam clay for detailing props, sculpting sections and filling in any seams or joins on props, much like with armour (see *A Guide to TV and Movie Cosplay*).

LARPers tend to use foam weapons so if you don't want to make one from scratch you can find a lot of good places online to buy convention-safe swords, shields, spears, and some other things beginning with 's' as well as pretty much any type of prop weapon you might need. Nerf Guns are also a good starting place for convention weapons that you can modify to look how you want. But remember to take the foam darts out. Convention security will not be happy with you shooting those all over the place!

Modifying any of these bought weapons can be very simple: just by rewrapping the handle in a different coloured fabric or giving it a paint job you can have the perfect prop for your costume. Or you can take it further, adding details and new elements like sword hilts or sights on guns until they are unrecognisable from where you started. The sky's the limit.

If you don't want weapon props you can still use foam, 3-D printing and other materials to make your props, though you may have less chance of finding a pre-made base for them online. However, many cosplayers have made patterns and instructions for a myriad of different props that you can find on YouTube, cosplay blogs (a good 'Google' can do no harm when you're starting a project), and on

forums and Facebook groups. You may not find exactly what you are looking for but patterns and techniques can be modified or repurposed to fit your needs once you have the basic idea.

The Puppet Show

Something else that is starting to be seen more and more as cosplay props, are puppets.

A lot of cosplayers get scared over the idea of making a puppet, worried that it is a massive undertaking. They envision Jim Henson style puppets or huge pieces like in *War Horse* rather than just going back to the bare bones of what puppetry is: breathing life into an object that wasn't there before. This can include using things like poi (swinging tethered weights) or fans or ribbon and silk twirling to represent magic, elemental powers, or similar. These are just as valid as puppet props as Kermit the Frog.

And even if you want a more traditional creature puppet, there are loads of different ways to make them, from the very complex, multi-jointed, massively movable things, all the way down to the super simple sock puppet that's been jazzed up a little. And all of them work so successfully as props. You can add an animal companion to your costume, maybe something like Haku's dragon

Onion Knight – *Dark Souls.*

form from Studio Ghibli's *Spirited Away* as a large scale arm/hand puppet, or bring a non-human character to life such as Olaf from *Frozen* as a muppet style puppet.

Puppetry can also be used to create wings, or a moving tail or even moving elements in wigs. You can use simple methods like hidden fishing wire (just give it a little pull and your wings will open) or more complex ones like motors and mechanisms. It's up to you and what you want to try.

It might sound complex but as with all the rest of cosplay, there are loads of tutorials out there to help you get started and walk you through step by step. There are some recommendations of places to look into at the back of this book for all of the different skills and ideas that are discussed.

But what about the next step, beyond the 'basic' prop build?

Upgrades People! Upgrades!

Cosplay is one of those things where there is always going to be more to learn. Whether it's because technology has moved forward and brought new and exciting crafting methods or materials into the world, or you discover a skill from a different time, place or culture that you have never heard of before. You will never run out of things to try, and that means you can always be looking to take your costuming talents to the next level.

If you are interested in the competitive side of cosplay, then adding more skills to your arsenal is a must. Being able to show off a technique that other people haven't used or is less well known in the cosplay community can put you in good stead for competitions, as not only does it show something unusual but also that you are someone who put thought and time into your work. It's bound to impress the judges.

But whether you want to compete or not, the creative drive to keep learning new skills can be an adventure for any cosplayer. Let's have a look at some of the techniques that you can use to push your cosplay to the next level.

Left, below and opposite: Cassandra – *Assassin's Creed: Odyssey.*

Fabric Upgrades

Fabric based skills like embroidery (both by hand and on machine), quilting, bead work, dyeing, and a multitude of other techniques – so many that there's no way I could list them all – can bring depth, details, and design intricacies to your costumes. Using techniques like this can add a new dimension to a costume, whether it has come from a 2-D, 3-D or physical reference.

Embroidery is often a great way to add more intricacy to a costume. You can do this by hand with traditional techniques, or do it on a machine, either by freehand stitching or using a programable machine to create your designs. Embroidery has a huge number of different techniques within it as well; it's not just stitched images or designs. There are so many separate types of stitching you can use, and different ways to use them that you could have made embroidery on two very different projects and have them almost unrecognisable from each other, other than both being sewn.

Using hand stitching can often look more old fashioned or magical and works really well for historical pieces and fantasy costumes. You could use it on a large-scale piece like Mollimaulk's coat from *Critical Role* or as a trim or decorative stitch just to add a little extra something to your costume. You could even include beads for just a touch more sparkle. It can take a long time and a lot of practice to get right, but the outcome is definitely worth it. Just don't push yourself too far and cramp your hands!

Mollymauk Tealeaf –
Critical Role Campaign Two.

A lot of costume designers use techniques like this in designs to show the character's personality and other important information about them on their clothing. Cersei from *Game of Thrones* has a lion embroidered onto one of her dresses that is made up of skull beads, which tells you a lot about her in a single glance. Cosplayers like to include those details when they recreate costumes, not just because it shows the skill of embroidery but also so that some understanding of the character can transition across into their own redesigns or original designs in the future.

Machine embroidery on the other hand is perfect for your more sci-fi, modern day, or more militaristic costumes to make patches, insignias or very large-scale pieces for garments. It's much quicker and because it's done on machine looks more modern.

You can see machine embroidered pieces in almost anything. Once you start seeing it on clothing, bags, patches, sashes, anything at all that can be sewn onto really, you'll be spotting it everywhere. It's very commonly used in the fashion industry and costume design. And while it might feel 'easier' to set off a machine to sew your design, and you can get premade designs that you just press 'go' with, there is a huge amount of skill in designing embroidery pieces for machine that should not be overlooked just because it's using technology. Creating the images, transferring them into a digital form that is compatible with your machine and then programming it to sew what you want all takes time and practice.

Mollymauk Tealeaf – *Critical Role Campaign Two.*

Freehand, or free machine, embroidery has a completely different look again. It's often much more organic, being done at speed it can sometimes get 'messy' and that can add a great deal of character and style to a piece. It can almost look like cobwebs or the markings on insects and animals – order within organic chaos.

This type of embroidery can also be used as a way of quilting, which can add texture and literal depth to your fabric. This is sewing three or more layers of fabric together to create a 3-D padded surface. It's used on a lot of period garments and winter jackets, as well as the traditional quilt blankets, but can definitely be used in your costumes. Although it can be a touch warm inside a quilted doublet.

Embroidery is something that can be added to almost any project and give it a little boost. There are no rules of how you have to use it. If it looks good, go for it and add that something extra to your costume.

Link and Sheik –
*The Legend of Zelda:
Ocarina of Time.*

If you want to add a design but either don't have access to an embroidery machine or don't feel up to spending the time doing a hand embroidered piece (fair enough, it can be daunting), then maybe try appliqué instead. This is a great way of creating designs and images on fabric, like a patch, by using fabric cut to the shape you want, fixed to the fabric of the garment with fabric glue or iron-on adhesive and then using a close zigzag stitch all the way around to attach it to the garment. You can layer fabric shapes, to make more detailed images or designs, attaching them together with the same method. It's a really great technique for bold designs like on a knight's tabard or a flag, or for making your own patches for a uniform of some sort; there are loads of ways you could use appliqué in your costumes.

If you want to add depth into the fabric itself without using sewing, then dyeing is the way forward. Having this skill in your bag will not only 'upgrade' your costumes when you use the fancier dyeing techniques, but being able to get the exact colour fabric you need for a costume makes life so much easier, especially since you can't always find what you need in the shops. A lot of cosplayers like to dye their own fabrics to get the right colour for a project but also to create effects of colour and texture.

When dyeing fabric you need to remember that natural fabrics will dye much more easily than human-made ones. Most human-made fabrics won't dye at all unless you use specialist dyes designed for them, which tend to be more expensive but are becoming a lot more accessible. With natural fabrics you can dye them with the dye you find in your local shops no trouble, and even use the natural dyes people would have used historically to create the colours and textures you want. And there are loads of interesting looks you can create with different ways of dyeing, and not just by making the whole piece of fabric one colour.

Ombre colouring is a very popular look for cosplays and can be achieved through dip dyeing or carefully spraying the fabric with a dye mixture.

Ice dyeing can create marbled, organic feeling colours on fabric, by piling ice onto prepared fabric, sprinkling the dye powder or solution onto the ice and then waiting for the ice to melt (normally over 24 hours). The results are magical.

You can also paint dye onto fabric and create patterns and images that way. This can be a little tricky, as the dye may bleed and spread into the fabric, but it does create some incredibly beautiful and intricate designs once you've got the hang of it.

Shay Cormac – *Assassin's Creed: Rogue.*

Or you could try batik: using wax to create patterns on plain fabric and then dyeing it another colour. Removing the wax with newspaper and an iron, you reveal the pattern in the original colour, contrasting with the dyed fabric.

If you want to push yourself in a different way, then you could consider learning to make your own patterns. Draping, block making and modifying patterns are all skills that can help you when costume making, even if you prefer using premade patterns. Being able to fit a pattern better to your body, change the sleeves or combine elements of different patterns together can be necessary when you're cosplayer, as half the time an exact pattern isn't going to look like that anime character that only turns up in one episode.

Props and Armour Upgrades

There are loads of skills that you can use to upgrade your armour and props work too. Adding detail to armour can take it from cool to straight up incredible with just a few techniques. Resin casting, foam clay sculpting, electronics and more can bring your costume pieces to life in a whole new way. And much like their fabric-based counterparts, they can be used in a multitude of different costumes. Neither fabric-based techniques nor props-based ones have to be strictly used in one type of costuming or one style of build, so having knowledge of skills across the board is helpful even if you prefer to stick with one build type over another.

Resin casting is super popular with cosplayers, hobbyists and artists. It's easy to get hold of supplies, though it can be a little pricey, and you can get all sorts of moulds, dye colours and inserts to make your resin pieces stand out from the crowd. A lot of cosplayers use resin for making gems and crystals to place into armour. *World of Warcraft* characters are very well known for having large inset gems in their armour for example, and resin gems, cast in silicon cupcake trays of all things, are the perfect shape.

Resin is incredibly versatile, going from clear to opaque whilst taking colour easily. It can also be used in a range of different sized moulds, so as long as you are willing to wait for a while for it to cure and harden you could make large scale resin pieces. However, it's good to bear in mind that the bigger you go the heavier it will be, so if you want to make a large gem or crystal it's better to go with something more like a coloured vinyl or even a plastic bottle heated up and reshaped with a heat gun.

If you are going to use resin please make sure you get the appropriate safety equipment as resin is toxic: a respirator mask (used for spray painting or wood work), replacement filters for the respirator, latex gloves, and safety goggles. You should also use it in a well-ventilated area or outside to keep the fumes away from you.

Another option for making gems and adding detailing is polymer clay.

Polymer clay is perfect for making custom rings, pendants, earrings and other little add-ons, but like resin the bigger the piece gets the heavier it will be. But unlike resin, you don't need a respirator to use it.

It is a cheap and easy way to add more to a costume. You can sculpt it with your hands or use tools for more refined designs. It comes in loads of colours, which you

Above and opposite:
Deathwing – World of
Warcraft.

can blend to get different shades or ombre effects, and it even has a translucent version. It's quick and simple to get it to cure: you just put it in the oven for about 35 minutes (check your clay's packaging for timings as this can vary), and boom! Done.

If you want to take your props even further, then one of the big additions to armour and props work that has been seen in all corners of the cosplay scene is adding lights and other electronics to your costumes. Making a light-up sword and putting a miniature smoke machine inside your armour can instantly take your costume to the next level.

It might seem complicated to do, but with a little time and some good tutorials – as ever, YouTube is the place to go for this, and Kamui Cosplay and others have some brilliant videos on the subject – you can start adding small electronic components to your costume without much hassle. Now that pinpoint LEDs, EL Wire and single LED pixels are readily available, both in shops and online, you can add lights without much thought at all. You can sew them into a garment, add them into the hilt of a dagger or set them inside a resin piece to make it glow! And you won't have to do anything more than change a battery.

The more you want to do and add the more complex it gets, but it is all perfectly doable if you take your time. Maybe you'll challenge yourself to have motorised wings next.

Wear, Tear and Weathering

Weathering can make your costume stand out in a crowd or give it a touch more realism. Ranging from subtle additions to make a costume look used or worn, all the way up to massive amounts of battle or 'adventure' damage, weathering can make a costume pop.

There are a lot of characters where you don't want to look as if your garments or armour are new off the shelf, so having a good selection of products on hand to add some of that 'just off the battlefield' realness is a must have for every cosplayer.

There are lots of ways to do this and you may find some products are suited more to one type of cosplay then another, so it's worth testing a few different techniques and products to find the perfect look for your costume. Just make sure you're experimenting on scraps!

Products to look into for weathering are:

- Charcoal (either to use as sticks to rub on or scraped down to powder to apply with a brush)
- Matte eyeshadows or contour (cheap and cheerful ones that you can ruin)
- Leather polish, paints or stain
- Acrylic paint and water mix (different consistencies for different effects)

- Fabric paints (again you can water these down for different looks)
- Marker pens (Copics or similar are great and Sharpies can be used, but you will need medical alcohol to blend them out)
- Inks and dyes (you can water them down for different effects)
- Dirty Down spray (comes in so many different 'dirt' types and colours)
- Fake blood or scab blood
- Food colouring or paints mixed with PVA glue
- Model making products (Tamiya have some great weathering products, the weather masters are brilliant for getting a good effect quickly, as are wargaming weathering paints)
- Sandpaper of different grades
- A lighter to burn edges (be VERY careful, you do not want to burn your costume!)

And of course:

- Actual mud, sand, dirt; why not drive a car over it in a pinch? (I've seen it done)

You'll need tools to apply your weathering as well. Things like make-up brushes and paint brushes of all sizes and texture (often an old ruined brush is better than a new

Chloe – *Detroit Become Human.*

one with weathering) are great for applying product to your costume. Or if you want to go a little more pricey, an airbrush can be worth the investment as it has all sorts of uses with cosplay, not just with weathering; such as general painting and applying body paints. Make sure you know which paint you are using though, as you don't want to stain your skin!

Cotton buds are really good for getting into all those cracks and crevices that a paint brush can't, and give an interesting texture as well. And kitchen paper is a must for dabbing, spreading and cleaning away excess product, especially with armour or props.

Whether you are working with fabric, foam, thermo-plastics or other materials the type/amount of weathering you put onto your costume will give a different look.

If your character has dragged themselves through a hedge backwards or worse, you might want to try heavier products like acrylic paints, leather stains and paints, dark or heavily applied charcoals, multiple layers of Dirty Down spray, or just throw everything you want at it.

For others, you will want a lighter, less aggressive touch to give their clothes a lived-in feel over something

Sam Vimes – *Terry Pratchett's Discworld.*

hyper dramatic. You can use inks and dyes of different strengths to add depth and wear to the fabric. Try twisting it up and submerging the fabric of garments to get a random feel or use a brush to get more colour and texture in certain areas. Lightly applied powders, airbrushed paint or just a couple of layers of Dirty Down are great to add to the edges or seams of garments.

Others will be somewhere in between or could vary from no weathering to being a beaten up pile of dirt. Have a play and see what looks good to you.

When weathering armour and props, techniques such as dry brushing are great for making anything look a bit worn and lend character instantly to any flat colour. Dry brushing is taking a tiny – like really tiny – amount of paint onto a clean dry brush and then quickly brushing it over an area. It works well to build up tone using a few different shades of paint on top of each other, darkest to lightest.

But if you want to add shadow or ingrained dirt you almost want to go the other way. Using watered down paint in a darker shade, sometimes even black, you want to work it into all the shapes, cracks and crevices of your piece. Then get dry kitchen paper and dab it up, leaving the paint in all the places you want to look dirty and pulling it off anywhere that should be cleaner. Repeat this until you are happy and then dry brush a lighter colour onto high points for extra depth.

Krem – *Dragon Age: Inquisition.*

Much as with fabric you can experiment and play around to your heart's content with different products, methods and levels of weathering. Once you've found what works for you, you'll be able to be as grubby as you want.

Once you've weathered your costume, it's time you weather you. It can ruin the illusion if you look fresh as a daisy in your beaten up costume, so adding some good old fashioned mud, blood and grime to yourself can pull the whole costume together. Just make sure you are using products designed to be used on skin and not acrylic paint though.

Matte powder contours and eyeshadows with a wet stipple brush or sponge can create great looking dirt ingrained into the skin, or use them on a toothbrush and splatter them across your face (similar to the popular freckles technique). Add more smears or splashes to make it look extreme. You can also use this make-up to create wrinkles, bruising, and general dirt smudges. Adding just a little pink and reddish brown under the eye and into the corner of it can automatically make you look more tired or ill, and you can add blues and purples if you want to really go for it.

If you want to spend a little more you can buy fake dirt online from film and theatre suppliers that's safe to use on your skin and will stay on all day.

Krem – *Dragon Age: Inquisition.*

Crème make-up/face paints work brilliantly as well. You can get general purpose ones from the high street as well as professional quality ones. There are some different types you can get with a range of colours for a range of weathering. You can get bruising pallettes with reds, browns, purples, blues, greens and even yellows to create realistic bruising, and which can be used as lightly or as heavily as you want. You can also use them to make a dried-on blood look.

If fake blood is what you want, it's super easy to get hold of and not expensive at all. Especially around Halloween. You can look at more expensive/professional products like scab blood and latex. If you want to make cuts, burns or other injuries use a product called rigid collagen for quick and easy scars on the skin.

Making great realistic weathering effects on your skin can be as simple or complex as you want to create the effect you want. As with the rest of cosplay, it's just experimentation and practice.

Ada Wong – Resident Evil Two.

Photoshoots and Videography

One of the best changes in cosplay in the last few years has been the increased popularity and quality of cosplay photography and videography. Everyone loves seeing great photographs and videos of their cosplays. It's one of the best feelings seeing those shots from conventions after you worked so hard on finishing your outfit. Long gone are the days when you had to hunt down a snap shot of your costume from the convention floor so you have proof you wore it. Now you can organise photoshoots with a range of different photographers and get high quality pictures of your hard work to show off on your social media platform of choice. You can also be included in cosplay music videos or event videos that will be being made at almost all conventions, though this is more of a game of chance than the organised shoots.

But these things aren't just happening at conventions anymore. People are setting up photo and video shoots on weekends for friends, or are paying for professionals. It's a whole new side to cosplay that lets you enjoy your hobby outside of the convention setting. As a community we are becoming more interested in taking things to the next level, and part of that is by doing these shoots, be that in studio or on locations rather than with that same bank of trees behind you at every event.

The results are often outstanding and really show the love for both craft and characters, as well as an appreciation for those with skills in videography and photography. However, setting up any type of shoot can be daunting, especially if you haven't done it before or are approaching a photographer or videographer you haven't worked with in the past. You may not have worked with anyone like that before!

But don't worry. You won't be the first or the last person needing a little nudge in the right direction when it comes to this sort of thing. There are plenty of ways to photograph and video your costumes and you can start wherever you feel comfortable.

Mettaton – *Undertale.*

Arranging a shoot

Whether you want to do a photoshoot or a video shoot there are a few different ways to go about arranging one:

You could message some friends and set it up yourselves in a local location or at home.

Toph Beifong –
Avatar: The Last Airbender.

This is a really good way to try out doing photoshoots or videos if you have never done one before and are a little nervous about being in front of the camera. You will be in a safe, supportive environment with people you know so it will be easier to relax and get used to the situation. It can be a little odd being the focus of the camera

after all. Working with your friends, you may not get the best results first time, but it's really fun, and you can get a feel for using the equipment. Collaborating together you can try new things, see what you can get out of using a phone vs using a high-tech camera, and learn about posing, composition and editing together. It's also free, and since cosplay is already an expensive hobby, you may not have the money to pay for a professional.

Messaging a photographer or videographer.

Talking with a photographer or videographer is a great way to set up a shoot. You may know of or be friends with someone trying their hand in this area or who is

Halloween Ana – *Overwatch.*

a professional. Chatting with them about setting up a shoot can be a great way to collaborate and produce a piece of work between you. If you don't know someone, don't worry. You can talk with a photographer or videographer you like through the online community or at a convention but be aware that there may be a charge for shoots. Many of them are freelancers and these things are their livelihoods so even if you are friends don't be offended or upset if they ask for some form of payment. If you have approached them with an idea, you are asking for a service from them, so you should pay for that. You can always discuss things such as 'Time for Prints' (both parties giving up time for the shoot and both being able to use the images for portfolios or similar, though this agreement will differ from person to person) or equivalent, collaborating on ideas together, but they are well within their rights to say no.

A photographer or videographer contacts you.

Sometimes photographers and videographers will message cosplayers they would like to work with, or chat with them at cons about ideas. This can lead to the same collaborative way of doing things as cosplayer contacting a photographer or videographer. And in that same regard, if someone contacts you to set up a shoot with you as the model or actor, you are more than allowed to say no at any point. Don't feel pressured into something you aren't comfortable with. Also do feel free to ask about things like travel costs and expenses. They have contacted you to work with them, so you can talk about these things with them. Collaboration is a two-way street. Assuming, however, that you are interested then go ahead and arrange the shoot, but make sure you put your safety first!

Security and safety on a shoot

If you are new to cosplay, or an old hand, there is a golden rule for when you are going on a shoot: take a friend/family member/chaperone, even if you know the person or people you are working with. This is by no means saying not to trust your photographer or videographer, far from it, but it is always better to be safe than sorry.

Make sure all the details of your shoot are arranged beforehand and that other people know where you (and your chaperone) are going to be and who with. If the photographer changes things last minute to something you aren't comfortable with – a different location, bringing another photographer without telling you, changing the type of shoot or anything else you aren't comfortable with – tell them and say no. If they aren't OK with that you can leave or cancel the shoot. Your comfort and safety are of a higher priority than getting photos of cosplay, no matter how good it is or how much you have planned. If you are made to feel in any way unsafe or uncomfortable on a shoot by the photographer, videographer or anyone else on the shoot, stop the shoot, tell them no and that you are uncomfortable. If this continues leave with your chaperone.

There can also be safety concerns with the physicality or 'stunts' being used in a photo or video shoot. Doing anything like using fire or smoke, getting into water such

Princess Allura – *Voltron: Legendary Defender*

as a river or lake, climbing up rocks/ruins/buildings/walls/other high objects, can be dangerous so make sure that you or the photographer/videographer (or both) know what they are doing and that it is safe. You should also have someone to help you with these types of 'stunts'. If you are going to be standing in a lake, have someone in wellies to help you get in and out. Having them there will also mean it's easy to remove yourself from the situation if needed, such as if something catches fire (and that is not a joke, it can happen). Being prepared for anything is better than things going wrong.

Lastly, if you are thinking about using any realistic prop weapons in public spaces, don't. Working somewhere with lots of people around when you are in cosplay draws attention, but you don't want to draw the wrong kind of attention by having a realistic looking gun, sword, or other weapon. At best you could scare people, at worst you could be arrested. If you are on a closed or private/limited access location then you can use what you want but if you are in a public space that will have members of the public in it, please take into consideration how you and the props you are using look to other people.

Princess Allura –
*Voltron: Legendary
Defender.*

A GUIDE TO MANGA, ANIME AND VIDEO GAME COSPLAY

Location hunting

Location hunting is one of the most fun, but also most stressful parts of any shoot. No matter if you are doing still photography or filming, have a single model or a large group, you are going to have to think seriously about your location. What do you want it to look like, what does it need to have in terms of accessibility and privacy, and how are you going to get there?

Searching around online can be great. Using Google maps and local photography and filming forums/sites can help you find cool places to get to, but often the best thing to do is walk or drive around your local area, seeing what you can find. There can be more than you think within walking distance, even in towns and cities. Or maybe you are just a short drive away from somewhere amazing that will work perfectly for your project. Plus if you drive you are forced to figure out the parking situation beforehand. Very useful!

It's a good idea to always be keeping an eye out for fun or exciting locations while you are out and about. You may not have a plan for a photoshoot right now, but you could need it in the future. Try to keep a catalogue of locations on your computer, or even in a physical binder so that you can always find somewhere you like. Snapping some quick pictures on your phone whenever you see somewhere you like is a great way of keeping a record, and is especially helpful if a location falls through and you have to replace it at short notice.

Sheik – *The Legend of Zelda: Ocarina of Time.*

One thing that is worth knowing is who owns the location you are looking at. Is it private land or public access? Public spaces you can turn up and, within reason, do what you want, but at any privately owned locations, for example land owned by English Heritage, the National Trust or similar, you will need to talk to their representatives about what is permitted on the site. A lot of the time it's common sense, but best to know if you are allowed to be shooting on the location. In all cases, be respectful.

Practice, Pose, Prepare

When you are planning or thinking about doing some form of shoot of a costume, knowing your character is even more important than when you are going to a convention. For conventions having a bank of three or four poses that you can break out the moment someone points a camera at you is great, but when you are on a photo or video shoot you will need a bit more. The likelihood is that you will be doing things that you wouldn't normally do for a quick snap at convention, using a terrain that challenges you, and the whole thing will allow for bigger and better expression of the character. Especially on a video shoot when you are acting rather than posing, studying your character's mannerisms and movement will mean that you get the result you want and that everyone involved is happy with.

You don't have to be an amazing actor to do shoots like this either. Take some time to think about the action and drama you want to portray and lock down those expressions and poses in the mirror. You can even practice with your phone camera so you know how you look and move. You may not be Oscar worthy, but you can nail the character with a little rehearsal.

It will also help to do some form of basic story boarding with your photographer or videographer. A quick look at the story you want to create, either in stills or video, gives you more consistency overall. This will help you not only visualise what you want, but also help your photographer understand what is in your head. Don't worry you don't have to be an artist. Stick figures will do, but a storyboard can also be achieved through Pinterest mood boards.

Left and opposite:
Scanlan and Pike –
*Critical Role Campaign
One.*

When working with anyone on a creative project you all need to be on the same page. There's no point making it harder for yourselves by going in blind. Spend some time discussing ideas, sending images that inspire you back and forth, looking at snippets from the source material that you want to recreate so that everyone involved can not only get their teeth into the project creatively but also make something that they are proud of. You're a team, so you need teamwork to get the best out of a shoot.

Side note for photographers/videographers

Cosplayers aren't always going to be models or find it easy in front of the camera for more than just a convention snap, so work with them. Be supportive and encourage them throughout the shoot. Give advice to help them think about the way they are posing, show them the pictures as you are taking them so you can illustrate what you mean, and remember, you can see what they are doing and they can't, so if their pose/facial expression isn't right let them know and suggest how they can fix it. Communication,

Reaper – *Overwatch.*

Thordak: The Cinder King – *Critical Role Campaign One.*

as ever, is key! And cosplayers, be supportive right back. The best work happens when everyone feels happy and supported in what they are doing.

Post shoot

It's no secret how hard it can be to wait for the results of all your hard work after a shoot, but unless you have paid you need to be patient. The photographer will do their best to get the images or video done as quickly as they can, but you can't demand things from the people you are working with.

When you do get to see the fruits of your labour, make sure that you leave watermarks on images or videos, and credit everyone involved in your shoot when you share your project online or elsewhere. You all worked hard on it, so you all deserve credit.

If you, the cosplayer, want to sell any photos as prints to your social media followers, that is something you will have to work out with the photographer. You may have to pay for the rights for the images. Something that many people don't know, is that the photographer owns the images unless you have a written contract/deal with them to the contrary. Under the law the copyright belongs to the person taking the picture, not the person in it.

Make sure that you read up on photography and videography law before you do your shoot so you know all the ins and outs of the legalities. This goes for both cosplayers and photographers.

Whether you are just doing a shoot with some friends or planning a whole film with a cast and crew, it's important that everyone involved is respected, knows how it's all going to work and what you plan to do with the project afterwards. Being safe and clued up on all of this will ensure that you have fun and create great work together.

The End?

Cosplay as a hobby can split into a myriad of things for the myriad of people involved. There will never be a right way to it, or that one perfect costume, because this is a constantly evolving hobby that pulls off in every which way imaginable, made up of all the different artistic ideas and styles of each individual cosplay. Do what you want to do, and how you want to do it. Admire the work people do but never believe that anyone is any better or any worse because of the stage they are at or the way they make their costumes. Respect the differences and praise creativity wherever you see it. Encourage others to try new things, and be encouraged to do those things yourself.

As a cosplayer you are bringing joy into your world and that leaks out into other people's. Play with what you do, tell the stories of the characters through your costumes, and embody the creativity, the positivity and what you love about the characters you cosplay. Have fun. In whatever way you want. That's all there is.

Image Copyrights

Cosplay Images
Megan Amis
Jemma Le Pelley

Historical Images
Carmen DiProspero
Aaron Pon
Edmund Hoff

References and Further Reading

Section 1: What is Cosplay?

What is Cosplay? Looking into the Hobby

Ashcraft, B. and Plunkett, L., 2014. *Cosplay World*. New York: Munich.

Crawford, G. and Hancock, D., 2019. *Cosplay And The Art Of Play*. 1st ed. Palgrave Macmillan.

Culp, J., 2016. *Cosplay*. Rosen Publishing Group, Inc.

Eder, D., Holyan, R. and Cajete, G., 2010. *Life lessons through storytelling*. Bloomington: Indiana University Press.

Birch, C., 1996. *Who says?* Little Rock: August House Publ.

Cohaku, The Cosplay Magazine, English Editions, Issues 1–5, https://www.cohaku.de/cohaku01-english/

The Cosplay Journal, Volumes 1–5, www.thecosplayjournal.com

Helen McCarthy, writer and historian, https://helenmccarthy.wordpress.com/

Sarkar, P., 2020. *History Of Cosplay*. [online] Vocal. Available at: https://vocal.media/geeks/history-of-cosplay

History of Cosplay

A Brief History of Manga

MacCarthy, H., 2014. *A Brief History Of Manga*. Lewes: Ilex.

Harding, C., 2021. *The Japanese: A History in Twenty Lives*. London: Penguin Books Ltd.

Hamada, N., 2013. *Manga: The Pre-History of Japanese Comics*. PIE Books; Illustrated Edition.

Manga into the Twentieth Century

Rousmaniere, N. and Matsuba, R., 2019. *Manga*. 1st ed. London: Thames & Hudson Ltd.

Mizuki, S. and Davisson, Z., 2014. *Showa 1938–1944*. Drawn & Quarterly.

Mizuki, S. and Davisson, Z., 2015. *Showa, 1953–1989*. Drawn & Quarterly; Illustrated edition.

Manga, Anime and Cosplay

Stuckmann, C., 2018. *Anime Impact: The Movies and Shows That Changed the World of Japanese Animation (Anime Book, Studio Ghibli, and Readers of the Soul)*. Mango.

Winge, T., n.d. *Costuming Cosplay*. 1st ed. Bloomsbury Visual Arts.

Phelan, E., 2020. *Cosplay: A 21st Century Form Of Escapism*. [online] Medium. Available at: https://medium.com/@EdwardPhelan1/cosplay-a-21st-century-form-of-escapism-2f8ea84f9c81

Clements, J., 2013. *Anime*. British Film Institute; 2013 edition.

Section 2: Where Do I Start?

Joicey, C. and Nothdruft, D., 2013. *How To Draw Like A Fashion Designer*. London: Thames & Hudson.

Kurtti, J., n.d. *The Art Of Disney Costuming*. 1st ed. Disney Editions.

Pollatsek, S. and Wilson, M., 2017. *Unbuttoned*. New York: Routledge.

Capaccio, N., n.d. *Costume Design In TV And Film*. Cavendish Square Publishing.

La Motte, R., n.d. *Costume Design 101 – The Business And Art Of Creating Costumes For Film And Television*. Michael Wiese Productions.

Clancy Steer, D., n.d. *Designing Costume For Stage And Screen*. Batsford Ltd.

Leese, E., 2013. *Costume Design In The Movies*. New York, NY: Dover Publ.

Section 3: Making Cosplay and What Happens Next

Wigs, and Make-up: Get the Full Look

Mango Sirene, *Mango Sirene Cosplay Channel*. [online] Youtube.com. Available at: https://www.youtube.com/user/MangoSirene

Online Kyne, *Online Kyne*. [online] Youtube.com. n.d. Available at: https://www.youtube.com/channel/UCPUBJHPd9AmO9n-xiT80QFw

Ruskai, M. and Lowery, A., 2015. *Wig making and styling*. Routledge.

Bouvet, M., 2019. *Practical Guide to Wig Making and Wig Dressing*. The Crowood Press.

Props: Weapons, Puppets, and the Pound Shop, Oh My!

Hart, E., 2017. *The Prop Building Guidebook, 2nd Edition*. 2nd ed. Routledge.

Thorsson, S., 2016. *Make: Props and Costume Armour*. San Francisco, CA: Maker Media, Inc (O'Reilly).

Quindt, S., 2016. *The costume making guide*. IMPACT Books; Illustrated edition.

Blumenthal, E., 2005. *Puppetry and puppets*. London: Thames & Hudson.

Currell, D., 1996. *An introduction to puppets & puppetmaking*. London: Quantum Books.

Upgrades People! Upgrades!

Ganderton, L., 2015. *Embroidery stitches step-by-step*. Penguin.

Hart, E., 2018. *The Prop Effects Guidebook*. 1st ed. Routledge.

Peacock, R. and Tickner, S., 2015. *Make & Mend*. London: Robinson.

Wear, Tear and Weathering

'...And Sewing Is Half The Battle!.' 2021. *Costume Weathering & Distressing Guide — '...And Sewing Is Half The Battle!'*. [online] Available at: https://www.andsewingishalfthebattle.com/costume-weathering-distressing-guide/

The Costume Rag. 2021. *How to Break Down Costumes for Maximum Effect – The Costume Rag*. [online] Available at: https://thecostumerag.com/break-costumes-maximum-effect/

Tested. 2021. *Weathering Techniques for Cosplay Costumes – Tested*. [online] Available at: https://www.tested.com/making/579789-weathering-techniques-cosplay-costumes/

Photoshoots and Videography

Stockman, S., 2011. *How to Shoot Video That Doesn't suck*. New York, NY: Workman Pub. Co.

DK, 2016. *Beginner's Photography Guide*. London: Dorling Kindersley Ltd.

Martin, K., 2019. *Creating cinematic cosplay photography — The Cosplay Journal*. [online] The Cosplay Journal. Available at: https://thecosplayjournal.com/articles-and-tutorials/creating-cinematic-cosplay-photography

Kerrigan, L., 2019. *A Cosplayer's Guide to Posing — The Cosplay Journal*. [online] The Cosplay Journal. Available at: https://thecosplayjournal.com/articles-and-tutorials/a-cosplayers-guide-to-posing